EXPLORING PASTON COUNTRY

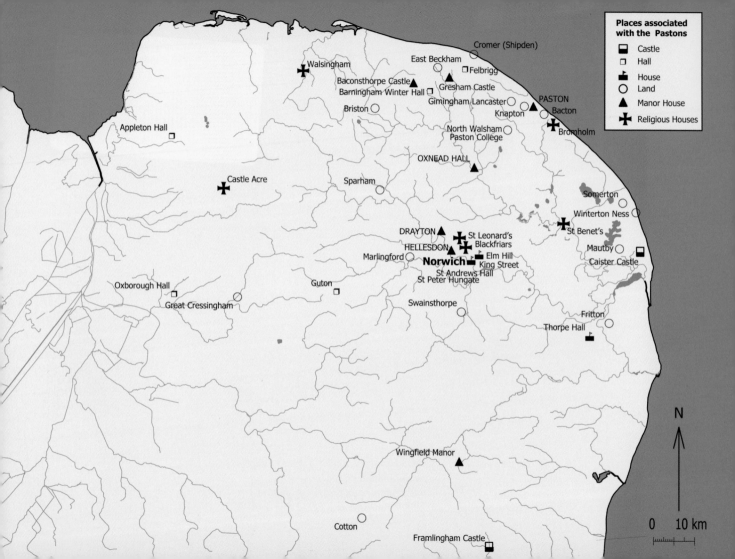

Places associated with the Pastons

- ▭ Castle
- ☐ Hall
- ⌐ House
- ○ Land
- ▲ Manor House
- ✠ Religious Houses

Cromer (Shipden)

Walsingham

East Beckham

Felbrigg

Baconsthorpe Castle
Barningham Winter Hall
Gresham Castle

Gimingham Lancaster

PASTON
Bacton

Briston

Knapton

Appleton Hall

North Walsham
Paston College

Bromholm

Castle Acre

Sparham

OXNEAD HALL

Somerton

Winterton Ness

St Benet's

DRAYTON
St Leonard's
Blackfriars

Mautby

HELLESDON

Caister Castle

Marlingford

Elm Hill
King Street

Norwich
St Andrews Hall
St Peter Hungate

Oxborough Hall

Guton

Swainsthorpe

Fritton

Great Cressingham

Thorpe Hall

Wingfield Manor

N

Cotton

0   10 km

Framlingham Castle

Exploring
Paston Country

POPPYLAND PUBLISHING

Lucy Care
with sketch maps by Jack Earl

Published by Poppyland Publishing, Cromer NR27 9AN

Design and typeset in 9.5 on 11.4 pt Imperial by Watermark, Cromer NR27 9HL

Printed by Barnwell's, Aylsham

The publication of this book has been assisted by a grant from the Norfolk Coast Partnership

Acknowledgements

Paston Heritage Society would like to thank their partners at Poppyland Publishing for joining them in this venture. Grateful thanks also to Siri Taylor of Argus publications who created the companion film *Paston Country: Pathways through Time* and to Tim Lenton who edited the original manuscript and walked the walks. Our sponsors, the Norfolk Coast Partnership, made the whole operation feasible and we received much help and encouragement also from Griffon Area Partnership.

Jack and Lucy would also like to thank their fellow committee members on the Paston Heritage Society for their warmth and encouragement even when bemused by our plans. Last but not least, this book is dedicated to Anne Earl and Simeon and Naomi Care who joined us on the picnics when we first went wandering in Paston Country.

Picture credits

Crabline Papers: page 64

Paul Damen: page 24 (bottom)

Alan M. Lowther: page 23 (right)

Paston Heritage Society (photos by Paul Damen): pages 11, 13, 22, 27 (main)

Christopher Pipe/Watermark: pages 21, 23 (left and centre), 24 (top), 26 (inset), 42, 43, 44, 45, 66

Paston Heritage Society collection: page 29

Paston Sixth Form College: pages 69, 70

Poppyland Photos: pages 3, 19, 26 (right), 46, 50, 51 (left), 53, 71, 73

All other photographs are the author's.

The map on page 9 is based on that by Christopher Barringer in *Exploring the Norfolk Town.* The map on page 48 is based on a base map licensed under the Creative Comons Attribution_Share Alike 2.0 licence by the OpenStreetMap project and its contributors

Contents

Pieces of Darkness

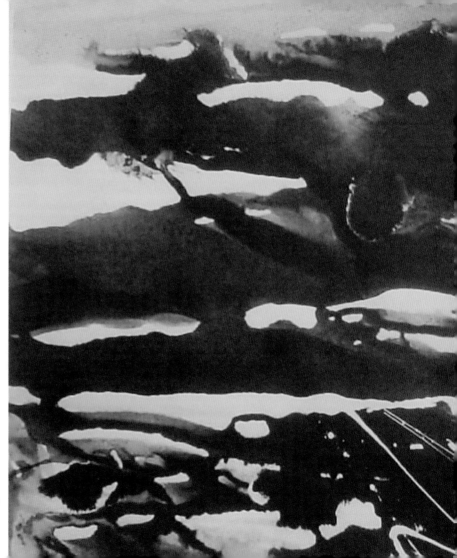

Hard towers penetrate the cloudburst Norfolk sky
high on high, forthright,
plying their inuksuk trade:
signposts for travellers in the mist and rain

Griffins crouch in the furrows behind the priory
and towards the silent sea
turning dreams to stone

There is mystery here

In the sacred sunken field a lower sentinel
among the huddled trees and lightning
guards instructions from another world:
words from the beginning
breath on breath, brooding
no longer quite secret

Footsteps are revealed
stealing through the subtle stubble
of history, blending into the landscape
hard to see
in any weather

Let there be light:
pieces of darkness
listen, but fail
to understand

Tim Lenton (artwork by Martin Laurence)

Introduction

This book is written from a compatriot's viewpoint. I would not have embarked on it if I did not live in Paston. I had studied the letters from a historian's point of view at university but had never really thought about the places they mention until I moved to Paston 20 years ago. Since then, guided by the letters, I have discovered the hidden memories of a whole people. Not just the Paston family but their friends, enemies and acquaintances are tantalisingly introduced in the documents comprising the Paston Letters, only to slip away.

Where can we find them? The answer for myself and for my father, Jack Earl, has been in their own *countrie*, as they referred to this corner of Norfolk. Here they are still spoken of fondly, as if they had only just left. Here the remnants of their grand estates remain, hidden in corners, overgrown and all but destroyed by ivy and that greedy hunt for building materials, especially stone, that characterises the history of building on a flint and clay soil. But it is all still there: we recognise the characters, the turns of phrase and the Norfolk landscape as shown in the letters. Walking around Paston, I see the rabbits, descendants of a royal warren; the windmill, once the site of Stow chapel; and the remnants of the king's road that the first William Paston caused to be moved to the north of the church.

As we have prepared the walks in this book, discovering more and more about this fascinating family as we go, we have also learnt more about the roots of Norfolk, for the Pastons were for a century the sole chroniclers of a lively period of history in Norfolk – and for two more centuries one of the most important families in the county. So this book is for those who, like the Pastons, love Norfolk and her countryside and for those who know that words come from people, and one cannot understand the letters without trying to understand the places and landscape the Pastons loved so well.

Lucy Care

Medieval Paston

The village of Paston stretches five miles inland from the North Norfolk coast between Bacton and Mundesley. It is mentioned in the Domesday book as Pastuna, and St Margaret's Church stands on the site of a former, possibly Anglo-Saxon church. One of the manors comprising modern Paston was the manor of Paston Sacre – the holy field. It may be because the church marks the holy field that, unlike its neighbours, it does not stand on a hill but in a secluded dip.

The village church was served by the monks of Bromholm priory in nearby Bacton. The monks owned most of the land but gave some at Paston to the Paston family, who, according to their own records, were descendants of William de Glanville, founder of the priory. Medieval Paston stood to the south of the church where the old road still lies beyond the lych gate in the churchyard. This road was closed to the villagers by act of parliament by William Paston I, the 'good' judge and the first Paston to leave the village, get an education and become a lawyer.

When the Pastons improved their property and built Paston Hall (where the new hall now stands), they no longer wanted their neighbours walking past the hall to the church. The church was the centre of village life, but the Pastons blocked the road to the churchyard and slowly moved their neighbours and tenants. Hall Farm remains near the church, but Green Farm, down on Paston Green, and The Limes Farm and Poplar Farm, on what was Paston Common, were built by the Pastons and remained in their hands until sold to Lord Anson in 1760.

One of the reasons the Pastons were able to rise in 100 years from poor farmers – even bondsmen (not free men) – to courtiers at the glittering Tudor court was that Paston lies between the lands of the powerful Dukes of Lancaster – over the boundary into Mundesley and beyond – and the lands owned by the Priors of Bromholm. Bromholm was not a powerful or rich house until about 1250, when it obtained its holy relic – the piece of the true cross, the Holy Rood of Bromholm. The majority of the land to the south belonged to the abbey of St Benet's at Holme, including parts of North Walsham. The remaining lands around Paston and Bacton were divided into a series of very small manors, easily bought up by the newly rich Pastons. Not that they relied solely on money: many small manors in Norfolk and beyond came to them by marriage. All Paston women were supposed to marry advantageously – for the good of the family.

The Pastons outgrew Paston and its hall as they grew richer and more important. The hall was where dowagers of the family lived, or children too small to introduce to polite society. It is where Christopher Paston lived – the son of William Paston. Declared an idiot and unable to inherit his father's estates in 1606, he represents the fruit of the curse of a long dead Prior of Bromholm that in every generation there would be a Paston of unsound mind. Elizabeth was incarcerated there by her mother Agnes for three months because she would not marry Scrope – 30 years her senior and hunch-backed into the bargain. Here Richard Calle the bailiff wooed the young Margery Paston and led her into an elopement leading to betrothal – a betrothal that the entire fury and might of the Paston family and the Bishop of Norwich could not shake. Here Margery sent her valentine, the first in the English language, to young John Paston III. From this little village the Pastons led their few serving men at arms to war

– to Barnet, or even to France and beyond. England was at war for the whole 100 years that the Paston family rose to power and riches, but the family never had a big army: Margaret Paston and her son, John, held Caister castle with a few men against the troops of the Duke of Norfolk – she lost, but they held out for three months.

At the back of Paston Church today stands the 15th-century coffer that once held all the church goods and papers. In coffers like this the Pastons, from William and Agnes on, stored every bit of paper they received – including the ones that said 'Burn this as soon as you have read it'. Their tombs stand in the church, and their names for centuries are recorded in the parish registers. Through their writings, which they never thought were to be published, we know more about the inhabitants of north Norfolk in the 15th century than at any time since.

In the Pastons' time, the road to Great Yarmouth ran along the cliff to the north of the holiday camp and inland to a crossroads at Stow mill. Here stood a chapel of rest (*stow* means rest) for pilgrims on their way to Bromholm priory.

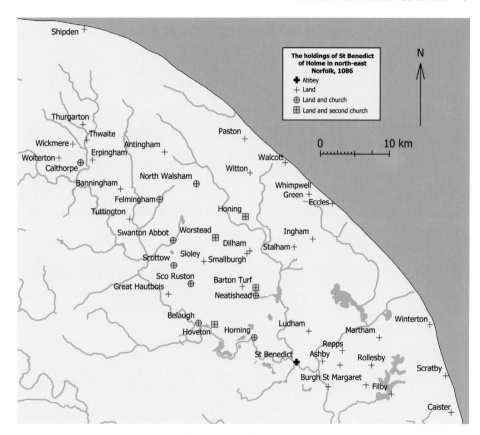

HOLDINGS OF ST BENEDICT (ST BENET'S) OF HOLME AS GIVEN IN THE DOMESDAY BOOK, 1086. THREE HUNDRED YEARS LATER, THESE WOULD FORM THE CORE OF THE PASTON FAMILY'S LANDS.

Inside the Paston Letters

Letter-writing in the 15th century was a costly and arduous process. Letters would be sent by hand, and messengers had to be paid. Most of the letters from Paston women were dictated rather than written by them, but it was Margaret Paston who was chiefly responsible for keeping and filing the letters carefully.

Here is a short letter in the original spelling from Margaret Paston to her husband, John I (all other letters have been modernised in spelling):

I am sory that ye xall not at hom be for Crystemes. I pray you that ye woll come as sone as ye may. I xhall thynke my-self halfe a wedowe be cause ye xal not be at home. God have you in hys kepyng. Wretyn on Crystemes Evyn. By you M.P.

William Paston, the 'good' judge, made over Paston Manor to Agnes, his wife, and it is mainly her letters that relate to Paston village and its neighbourhood.

There was a great dispute at Paston about a wall which Agnes had built to stop an alleged right of way running through the grounds of her manor. Here she reports to John on the matter:

I greet you well, and let you weet that on the Sunday before Saint Edmund, after evensong, Agnes Ball came to me to my closet and bade me good even, and Clement Spicer with her. And I asked him what he would; and he asked me why I had stopped up the King's way. And I said to him I stopped no way but mine own, and asked him why he had sold my land to John Ball; and he swore he was never accorded with your father. And I told him if his father had do as he did, he would a be ashamed to a said as he said.

And all that time Warren Harman leaned over the parclose and listened what we said, and said that the change was a ruely change, for the town was undo thereby and is the worse by £100. And I told him it was no courtesy to meddle him in a matter but if he were called to counsel. And proudly going forth with me in the church, he said the stopping of the way should cost me 20 nobles, and yet it should down again. And I let him weet he that put it down should pay therefor. Also he said that it was well done that I set men to work to

owl money while I was here, but in the end I shall lose my cost. Then he asked me why I had away his hay at Walsham, saying to me he would he had wist it when it was carried, and he would a letted it; and I told him it was mine own ground, and for mine own I would hold it; and he bade me take four acre and go no farther. And thus shortly he departed fro me in the churchyard.

Agnes had a pragmatic view of her children: they were for the most part considered to be property for the family as was usual for that time. They were expected to be obedient and extremely respectful towards their parents, even in adulthood. In this letter, written by Elizabeth Clere to John Paston I, we read how Agnes treated Elizabeth, her daughter, when she refused to marry Stephen Scrope.

And if ye can get a better, I would advise you to labour it in a short time as ye may goodly, for she was never in so great sorrow as she is nowadays; for she may not speak with no man, whosoever come, ne not may see ne speak with my man, ne with servants of her mother's but that she beareth he on hand otherwise than she meaneth. And she hath sin Easter the most part be beaten once in the week or twice, and sometime twice in a day, and her head broken in two or three places.

AGNES PASTON'S SEALS AFFIXED TO A MORE FORMAL DOCUMENT

Wherefore, cousin, she hath sent to me by Friar Newton in great counsel, and prayeth me that I would send to you a letter of her heaviness, and pray you to be her good brother, as her trust is in you.

Cousin, I pray you burn this letter, that none of your men may see it; for it my cousin, your mother knew I had sent you this letter she wouldn't love me again.

In 1459 Margery Paston, another recalcitrant daughter, secretly married the Paston bailiff, Richard Calle. Every effort was made by the family to have the marriage put aside because she had demeaned both herself and her family, and lost the family the chance of a valuable marriage settlement. Here Margaret Paston recounts the church's efforts to have the marriage put aside:

On Friday the Bishop sent for her by Ashfield and other that arn right sorry of her demeaning. And the Bishop said to her right plainly, and put her in remembrance of how she was born, what kin and friends that she had, and should have mo if she were ruled and guided after them, and if she did not, what rebuke and shame and loss it should be to her if she was not guided by them, and cause of forsaking of her for any good or help or comfort that she should have of them; and said that he had heard say that she loved such one that her friends were not pleased with that she should have, and therefore he bade her be right well advised how she did, and said that he would understand the words that she had said to him, whether it made matrimony or not. And she rehearsed what she had said, and said if tho words made it not sure she said boldly that she would make it surer ere than she went thence; for she said she thought in her conscience she was bound, whatsoever the words wern. These lewd words grieve me and her grandma as much as all the remnant And the Bishop and the chancellor both said that there was neither I nor no friends of hers would receive her.

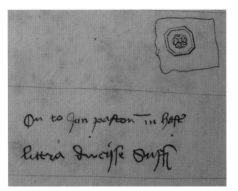

COVER OF A LETTER WRITTEN TO JOHN PASTON 'IN HAST'

And then Calle was examined apart by himself, that her words and his accorded, and the time and where it should a be done. And then the Bishop said that he supposed that there should be found other things against him that might cause the letting thereof, and therefore he said he would not be too hasty to give sentence thereupon and said that he would give over day till the Wednesday or Thursday after Michaelmas, and so it was delayed. They would an had their will performed in haste, but the Bishop said he would none otherwise than he had said.

I was with my mother at her place when she was examined, and when I heard say what her demeaning was I charged my servants that she should not be received in mine house.

The quarrel was evidently made up, however, as Richard Calle continued to be the bailiff and Margaret Paston bequeathed:

To John Calle, son of Margery my daughter xxli, when he cometh to the age of xxiii year. And if the said John dye or he cometh to the said age, then I wulle that the seid xxli evenly be divided attwenn William and Richard, sones of the seid Margery.

The letters were mostly written during the Wars of the Roses but surprisingly few deal with happenings outside the circle of the Pastons. Here is an account of the execution of the Duke of Suffolk in 1450:

Right worshipful sir, I recommend me to you, and am right sorry of that I shall say, and have so wesh this little bill with sorrowful tears that uneaths ye shall read it.

As on Monday next after May Day there came tidings to London that on Thursday before the Duke of Suffolk came unto the coasts of Kent, full near Dover, with his two ships and a little spinner; the which spinner he sent with certain letters, by certain of his trusted men, unto Calais ward, to know how she should be received. And with him met a ship called Nicholas of the Tower, with other ships waiting on him and by them that were in the spinner the master of the Nicholas had knowledge of the Duke's coming. And when he espied the Duke's ships he sent forth his boat to weet what they were, and the Duke himself spake to them and said he was by the King's commandment sent to Calais ward, &c. And they said he must speak with their master; and so he, with two or three of him men, went forth with them in their boat to the Nicholas. And when he came the master bade him 'Welcome, traitor,' as men say; and further, the master desired to weet if the shipmen would hold with the Duke, and they sent word they would not in no wise; and so he was in the Nicholas till Saturday next following.

Some say he wrote much thing to be delivered to the King, but that is not verily know. He had his confessor with him, &c. And some say he was arraigned in the ship, on their manner, upon the apeachments, and found guilty, &c.

Also he asked the name of the ship, and when he knew it he remembered Stacy, that said if he might escape the danger of the Tower he should be safe; and then his heart failed him, for he thought he was deceived.

And in the sight of all his men he was drawn out of the great ship into the boat, and there was an axe and a stock; and one of the lewdest of the ship bade him lay down his head, and he should be fair ferd with, and died on a sword; and took a rusty sword, and smote off his head within half a dozen strokes and took away his gown of russet and his doublet of velvet mailed, and laid his body of the sands of Dover. And some say his head was set on a pole by it, and his men set on the land by great circumstance and prayer. And the sheriff of Kent doth watch the body, and sent his undersheriff to the judges to weet what to do, and also to the King. What shall be do further I wot not, but thus far is it: if the process be erroneous, let his counsel reverse it, &c.

As for all your other matters, they sleep; and the friar also, &c.

Sir Thomas Kyriell is take prisoner, and all the leg harness, and about three thousand Englishmen slain. Matthew Gough with fifteen hundred fled, and saved himself and them; and Piers Brusy was chief captain, and had ten thousand Frenchmen and more, &c.

I pray you let my mistress your mother know these tidings, and God have you all in his keeping. I pray you this bill may recommend me to my mistresses your mother and wife, &c. James Gresham hath written to John of Damme, and recommendeth him, &c. Written in great haste at London the 5 day of May, &c.

By your wife, W.L.

The Paston family were given permission to have a chapel in their new manor of Paston. The church was cared for by the monks of Bromholm at Bacton. It was common at the time for families to have a domestic chaplain and, of course, it gave the Pastons freedom from the priors of Bromholm in the matter of

PART OF A PASTON LETTER IN THE ORIGINAL WRITING

worship. As can be seen from this excerpt, the blocking of the procession way to the church from the manor was another factor in the wall dispute.

I spake this day with a man of Paston side, and he told me that a man of Paston told him that Paston men would not go procession father than the churchyard on St. Mark's day; for he said the procession-way was stopped in, and said within short time men hoped that the wall should be broke down again.

The Pastons were a devout family, and the letters made many references to pilgrimages and are often dated by the ecclesiastical calendar.

Here John Paston II writes after the death of John Paston I, whose body he wished to bring home to be buried at Bromholm. He did achieve this, and the tomb was moved to Paston Church after the dissolution of the monasteries and the decay of Bromholm Priory:

Right worshipful mother, after all duties of humble recommendation, as lowly as I can, I beseech you of your daily blessing and prayer.

Please it you to understand that whereas ye willed me by Poyness to haste me out of the air that I am in, it is so that I must put me in

God; for here must I be for a season, and in good faith I shall never, while God sendeth me life, dread more death than shame. And thanked be God, the sickness is well ceased here, and also my business putteth away

my fear. I am driven to labour in letting of the execution of my unkind uncle's intent, wherein I have as yet none other discourage, but that I trust in God he shall fail of it.

A Norfolk Valentine

In long established Norfolk families to this day, St Valentine has a special place. He brings small presents for the family on 14th February, especially to the children. A mysterious knock on the door or ring of the bell, after dark, will bring the children running to the door. The shy saint always leaves something. It is therefore fitting that the first recorded Valentine should come from a Norfolk family. Here Dame Elizabeth Brews writes to John Paston III in February 1477:

And, cousin, on Friday is St Valentine's day, and every bird chooses for himself a mate; and if you like to come on Thursday night and arrange that you may stay until Monday, I trust to God that you may speak to my husband, and I pray that we may bring the matter to a conclusion.

And here is Margery's letter the same month:

And, if it please you to hear of my welfare, I am not in good health of body or heart, nor shall be until I hear from you. For there knows no creature what pain I endure, and I should rather die than dare it discover. And my lady, my mother, has argued this matter with my father full diligently, but she can get no further than you know of, for which, God knows, I am full sorry. But, if you love me, as I trust you do, you will not leave me there. For if you had not have the livelode that you have, and I had to work as hard as any woman alive might do, I would not forsake you. My heart me bids ever more to love you truly over all earthly things. I beseech you that this bill be not seen by any earthly creature save only yourself.

The Letters and John Fenn

I have spoken to my Lord of Ely divers times, which hath put me in certainty by his word that he will be in with me against mine uncle in each matter that I can show that he intendeth to wrong me in; and he would fain have a reasonable end betwixt us, whereto he will help, as he saith. And it is certain my brother, God have his soul, had promised to abide the rule of my Lord Chamberlain and my Lord of Ely. But I am not yet so far forth, nor not will be, till I know my Lord Chamberlain's intent; and that I purpose to do to-morrow, for then I think to be with him, with God's leave. And since it is so that God hath purveyed me to be the solicitor of this matter, I thank Him of His grace for the good lords, masters, and friends that He hath sent me, which have perfectly promised me to take my cause as their own, and those friends be not a few.

These few excerpts give some idea of the content of the Paston Letters. For further reading *The Paston Letters* are available in a number of editions (see page 76).

The bulk of the letters and papers were sold by William Paston, 2nd Earl of Yarmouth, the last representative of the family, to the antiquary Peter Le Neve early in the 18th century. According to Fenn's introduction to the letters, on Le Neve's death in 1729 they came into the possession of Thomas Martin of Palgrave, who had married his widow; and upon Martin's death in 1771 they were purchased by John Worth, a chemist at Diss, whose executors sold them three years later to John Fenn of East Dereham.

John Fenn was an antiquary. He saw his chance to add something new to contemporary understanding of 15th-century England. As he says:

The sufferings of warriors, the distresses of private life, occasioned by so tempestuous a season, and the concise rapidity of the narratives, will present a truer picture of that turbulent period than could be exhibited by the artful pencil of a sedate historian.

He also saw his big chance to achieve an outstanding piece of scholarship. His plan was careful, well researched and was to inspire scholars not only of social and political history but of the history of the development of English as a language, the development of watermarks and paper production and of calligraphy. As he remarked in his introduction:

a faithful delineation of our language, during a period of almost half a century, in an age too, famous for little besides its barbarity and civil dissensions, is a matter not only of much curiosity but of some use.

He concentrated on letters relating to the court and to the political life of the period because he felt that only the history of great events and noble people would be of interest to his audience. But later generations find the thoughts and reflections on the everyday lives of the Pastons and their neighbours a window into an extraordinary time - made understandable by the very ordinary emotions and reactions recorded in the letters.

The first edition of the letters sold out in a week. Fenn gave copies to carefully selected members of the great and good, including Boswell and Johnson, and of course the king, to whom he dedicated his work. The Norfolk Record Office has a file of some of the letters written to Fenn in response to publication. To us, some of the reactions seems overstated and extraordinary – 'They cause me to forget to eat or sleep' (W. Hutton) – but we forget that since their discovery the letters have been a major research source for historians of the period and have thus informed much of our reading of the period.

Fenn not only transcribed the letters, first as written and then in the language of 1787; he also saw the importance of reproducing each signature on the letters, the incidental doodles, like a floor plan of Gresham castle, the seals and watermarks and, in later editions, reproductions of how the letters were folded, sealed and addressed. He states,

The paper on which they are written, is of different degrees of fineness; some sheets being rough, and, what we now call very coarse, while others are perfectly smooth, and of a much finer texture, however must all have been of foreign manufacture since the art of papermaking was not introduced into England before the reign of Henry VII.

He carefully includes the eight-pointed star of John Tate, the first English papermaker and the man who made the introduction

SOME WATERMARKS IN THE PAPER USED BY THE PASTONS, AS REPRODUCED IN JOHN FENN'S EDITION.

to England of the first printing press by Caxton, a viable possibility, for apart from convenience, England was at war and importing paper from the continent was a tricky and expensive business.

In 1787 Fenn published his first two volumes. He had 500 copies printed, with each frontispiece hand coloured (for which he paid the artist seven shillings). A second edition appeared shortly afterwards. In 1789 Fenn published two other volumes of letters, and when he died in 1794 he had prepared for the press a fifth volume, which was published in 1823 by his nephew, Serjeant Frere. On 23rd May 1787 Fenn was knighted; his

neighbour J. Allen, rector of East Dereham, wrote:

Happy do you feel yourself that the parade of yesterday is over. Yet few authors have attended at St James, (to receive a knighthood), with a Prime Minister to lessen the embarrassment of introduction. I went instantly with your letter to Mrs Fenn.

In gratitude for the honour, John Fenn presented the originals of his first two volumes to George III. These manuscripts soon disappeared, as did the originals of the three other volumes. This caused doubt as to the authenticity of the work, but the matter was resolved when some of the original manuscript resurfaced.

The papers published by Fenn did not, however, comprise the whole of the Paston Letters. When the 2nd Earl of Yarmouth died in 1732 other letters and documents relating to the Pastons were found at Oxnead, and some of these came into the hands of Francis Blomefield; some of these were acquired by the antiquary John Ives. Most of the Paston letters and documents are now in the British Library, but others are at Orwell Park, Ipswich; in the Bodleian Library, Oxford; at Magdalen College, Oxford; and a few at Pembroke College, Cambridge.

The Paston family tree

An abridged version showing the relationships of Paston people mentioned in this book

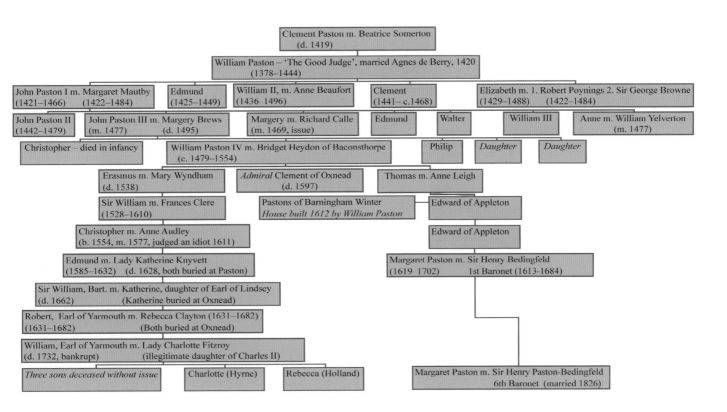

Clement Paston m. Beatrice Somerton
(d. 1419)

William Paston – 'The Good Judge', married Agnes de Berry, 1420
(1378–1444)

John Paston I m. Margaret Mautby   Edmund   William II, m. Anne Beaufort   Clement   Elizabeth m. 1. Robert Poynings 2. Sir George Browne
(1421–1466)   (1422–1484)   (1425–1449)   (1436–1496)   (1441– c.1468)   (1429–1488)   (1422–1484)

John Paston II   John Paston III m. Margery Brews   Margery m. Richard Calle   Edmund   Walter   William III   Anne m. William Yelverton
(1442–1479)   (m. 1477)   (d. 1495)   (m. 1469, issue)   (m. 1477)

Christopher – died in infancy   William Paston IV m. Bridget Heydon of Baconsthorpe   Philip   *Daughter*   *Daughter*
(c. 1479–1554)

Erasmus m. Mary Wyndham   *Admiral* Clement of Oxnead   Thomas m. Anne Leigh
(d. 1538)   (d. 1597)

Sir William m. Frances Clere   Pastons of Barningham Winter   Edward of Appleton
(1528–1610)   *House built 1612 by William Paston*

Christopher m. Anne Audley   Edward of Appleton
(b. 1554, m. 1577, judged an idiot 1611)

Edmund m. Lady Katherine Knyvett   Margaret Paston m. Sir Henry Bedingfeld
(1585–1632)   (d. 1628, both buried at Paston)   (1619 1702)   1st Baronet (1613-1684)

Sir William, Bart. m. Katherine, daughter of Earl of Lindsey
(d. 1662)   (Katherine buried at Oxnead)

Robert, Earl of Yarmouth m. Rebecca Clayton (1631–1682)
(1631–1682)   (Both buried at Oxnead)

William, Earl of Yarmouth m. Lady Charlotte Fitzroy
(d. 1732, bankrupt)   (illegitimate daughter of Charles II)

Three sons deceased without issue   Charlotte (Hyrne)   Rebecca (Holland)

Margaret Paston m. Sir Henry Paston-Bedingfeld
6th Baronet (married 1826)

Mundesley to Paston

3 – 4 miles (circular walk)

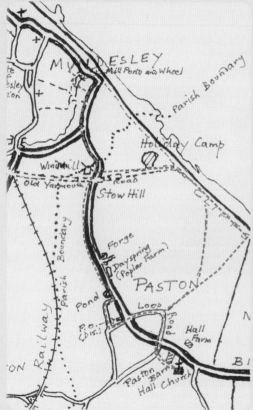

¶ Park at the main car park on the seafront. Walk out of the car park at the rear, and you will reach Gold Park. Turn left, then right at the corner of the park turn right, and you will find yourself on a short narrow path. This emerges into a wider unmade road. About 30 yards on, opposite Meadow Drive turn left down a narrow paved path, which emerges on Beckmeadow Way (though this is not signposted). Turn right and after about 100 yards left down a wide road (still un-made), which emerges at the Royal Hotel. Turn right and walk uphill to Stow Wind-mill. *The windmill is open to visitors and has a café in summer and at weekends. It is on the site of Stow Chapel.*

¶ From the windmill, cross the road and walk down to the clifftop past the holiday camp. *The holiday camp is one of the oldest in Britain; it is on the site of the old Brick Kilns for Mundesley and Paston. You are now walking on the Old Yarmouth Road – much of it has disap-peared into the sea, but it was how the Pastons would have got down to their*

great castle of Caister. Interestingly enough the old cross at Stow Chapel and the stone crosses at Southrepps and Gresham form a straight line with this road. Was it the pilgrim route between Walsingham and Bromholm priories? The clifftop marks the remains of Paston common land. Even in the times of the Pastons, residents complained they should not have to pay so much rent when their fields had fallen into the sea.*

¶ You now have a choice of routes. You can follow the Paston Way, an (unmarked) per-missive footpath, approached by a track that goes straight on where the cliff path turns left and then, as a narrow footpath, goes right and left round a field before heading straight towards Paston Church in the distance. Or keep on the cliff path until you get to the corner of Bacton gas site and turn right. *You are now walking at an angle to the gas site up the remains of Craft Lane, the village's main access to the cliff from this end of the village until the gas site was built. There is a beautiful panoramic view from the cliff down Paston Way. It is possible to see six churches, Trimingham golf ball (MOD), Happisburgh lighthouse and, of course, Bacton gas site and get a real sense of the light and landscape that make this coast unique.*

¶ At the end of these paths (they meet at

the end of Craft Lane), turn left and walk down to the end of the loop road. *This used to be the main village street.*

¶ Cross at the crossroads and walk down past the end of the Great Barn. Here you turn left and walk across the barn's stack yard. *The new pathway opens officially in 2010; until then, walkers use it at their own risk.*

The footpath leads to the churchyard, passing the Great Barn on your left. *The present church is on the site of an Anglo Saxon church mentioned in the Domesday book.*

¶ On leaving the church, take the same footpath back past the barn and walk up to the crossroads and over the main road to the loop road. Walk right round the loop road and you will pass Peacock Hall – the Old Rectory – on your right.

Recross the main road to the post box and telephone kiosk and continue down Chapel Road. *The almshouses are on your right.*

¶ At the bottom of Chapel Road turn right past the recreation ground and up the hill – yes, it is called Paston Hill on old maps! *This is Bears Road – possibly after a Mr Bear, but more likely because a bear was once found in a ditch here. A circus used to have a touring show at Mundesley and walked the animals*

The Almshouses

Sir William Paston in his will of 1610 left two houses at Paston for the poor of the parish. In 1832 the churchwarden stated that 'the debt incurred by building at the Town House is paid off, the rent of eight acres, one rood and 20 perches [3.4 ha] of land shall be applied for the benefit of poor persons not parish paupers and the Town House or almshouses appropriated for the residence of poor persons' – so it appears that the brick half of the almshouses was constructed only in 1832. The flint half has the garden containing the well, presumably shared. The architecture of the flint house is very like that of the outhouses to the Great Barn. The tiled floor and window frames are very similar.

Each house consists of two rooms with tiled floor and a small fireplace in one room. There is an earth closet in the garden. The rent was one shilling (5p) a year, and the flint cottage was occupied until recently. The almshouses became a liability as early as 1902: the rent was so small, there was no money to pay the rates, and the trustees were asked to pay – and refused point blank. They were next advised to 'take advantage of the present rise in price of land next the coast to effect an advantageous sale'. But the houses remain the property of the village, renovated and maintained to a high standard and still available for the poor.

up to Paston Pond for water. *The bear seems to have expired and been left here.*

¶ Turn left past Paston Pond and take the new footpath running alongside the road. *The old village pound is concealed in the bushes opposite the pond – it is triangular in shape. It is worth pausing to look at the Forge on your right where Frank Gray lived and England Mason worked. It still has the*

original anvil in use, but now makes rather beautiful ironwork.

¶ *The path leads straight down to Mundesley past Stow Mill.* Now retrace the beginning of the walk to the car park – or, if you wish, follow the footpath towards the school and then continue left along the road, turn right and right again into the town, heading for the sea front.

St Margaret's Church

The present church was built around 1350. There is a round of flints to the north-east of the chancel in the graveyard, thought variously to be the base of a cross or the tomb of an unknown sailor washed up on the beach and buried by the villagers. The churchyard is a sea of snowdrops and wild daffodils in spring, and very pleasant at any time of the year.

The original entrance to the churchyard was through the lych gate. William Paston had a wall built across the 'king's way' – the old village street – and moved the road to the north of the church. The way still exists. It was preserved as the carriageway to Paston Hall and comes out on the Bacton road.

Inside the church, look for the 15th-century coffer and the wall paintings: St Christopher and the more unusual old French legend of the three kings. St Christopher was said to be the friend of all who labour; to look upon his likeness was to be immune that day from mischance, and he was 'greatly invoked in times of pestilence' – little wonder that his picture, so often drawn on the walls of 14th- and 15th-century churches, had its position opposite the main entrance.

In the Paston painting, unfortunately, the giant's right arm and all but the top of the staff are missing, but fish swim in the water. The Child is holding the orb in the left hand; the right arm is extended and the fingers on the hand are in the position of blessing, while the foot fully drawn has six toes. The figure is 12 feet (3.6m) high. This painting, of 14th-century date, was partly hidden under plaster.

A little further to the east on the same wall

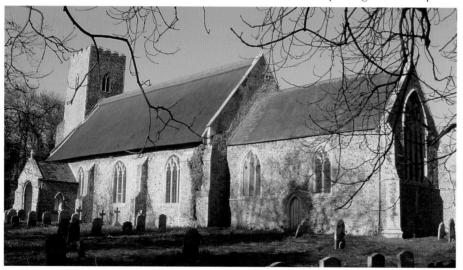

three skeletons are depicted. This is one of the panels illustrating an old French morality tale, *Les trois vifs et les trois morts* (the three living and three dead), a legend of three kings who in a merry mood while hunting in a forest were suddenly confronted with three skeletons hanging. The painting is well preserved.

The fragment immediately below the three figures – the hind part of an animal backed by a robed figure – belongs probably to a painting of the *Doom*, or *Last Judgement*. Below the skeletons is a small kneeling figure.

No doubt both north and south walls were covered with painting 'for instruction and admonition' (the south wall has not been thoroughly examined). Splashes of heavy red paint show how one work has been destroyed.

To the left of the pulpit is the old rood screen stair entrance where, when the organ was moved during restoration of the church in the 1920s, books and papers were found dating back to the 15th century. Most of these are now in the Norfolk Record Office; the most moving items for me are the 15th-century service sheets – using the book of Judith – beautifully illuminated but then cut and folded to make a cover for the first Paston

ST CHRISTOPHER CARRIES THE INFANT CHRIST ACROSS A RIVER, WHILE (INSET LEFT) FISH SWIM IN THE WATER AROUND HIS FEET.

register. Much handled, it has a patina of many fingers and even graffiti from 400 years ago, when illuminated manuscripts were no longer treasured by the church.

BELOW: ENTRANCE TO THE OLD ROOD STAIRS, WHERE OLD PARISH RECORDS AND PRE-REFORMATION SERVICE SHEETS (PICTURED RIGHT) LAY FORGOTTEN FOR CENTURIES.

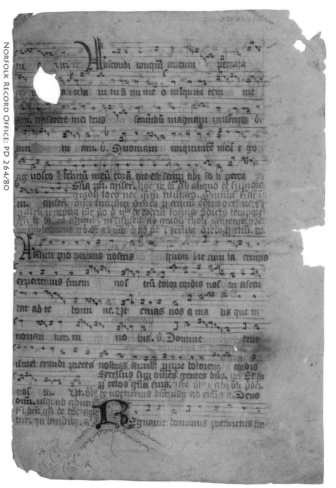

NORFOLK RECORD OFFICE: PD 264/80

Take time to look at the boards showing past vicars at the back of the church, as well as the Paston tombs at the east end. Here are recorded all who served Paston church: monks of Bromholm up to the Reformation and headmasters of Paston Grammar School after its founding by William Paston in 1620. Paston did not have a resident vicar until the coming of the Paston Mack family, who bought the estate because they claimed descent from the Pastons, and who restored the church. Their tragic story is told in the stained glass windows and war memorials. Their ownership of the hall did not survive two world wars, although their descendants still live in the village.

KATHERINE PASTON, RIGHT, BORN A KNYVETT, LIVED AT PASTON HALL WITH HER HUSBAND SIR EDWARD, EVEN AFTER SIR EDWARD HAS INHERITED THE FAMILY ESTATES INCLUDING THE SUMPTUOUS OXNEAD HALL. AFTER HER DEATH, THEIR SON WILLIAM HAD A WONDERFULLY ORNATE MONUMENT MADE TO HER MEMORY BY NICHOLAS STONE. IT INCLUDES A VERSE BY JOHN DONNE. STONE WAS PAID £340 AND WAS 'VERY EXTREORDIENERLY ENTERTAINED THAR'.

SACRED
To the Memory of
JOHN RISING,
Who died July 10th 1810,
Aged 65 Years.
Also of
ELIZABETH his Wife
Who died August 20th 1844
Aged 97 Years.

IN PASTON CHURCH WILL ALSO BE FOUND BENCH-ENDS (FAR RIGHT) CARRYING THE PASTON ARMS, AS WELL AS THE USUAL RANGE OF LOCAL FAMILY MEMORIALS (AS ABOVE).

The names of past villagers – Lee, Rising, Harman, Purdy, England Mason the blacksmith, the millers, the Gaze family – survive on the bell ringers' boards, the tombstones and war memorials. In this church we can see that time does not change the essential nature of village life, where gossip, recipes and rumours still run through the networks without the benefit of email and the internet. The circular bench near

the road, and the church gates, were made at Paston forge by the present blacksmith. The forge, the farms, the almshouses and the Great Barn have survived where the Pastons could not.

The Great Barn at Paston

The Paston Great Barn was built by William Paston in 1581. It is over 164 feet (about 50m) long and is one of the largest in the

county. The inscription with the date of the barn is over the small north-west door. There is another inscription plate on the north side above the road.

It is likely that the stone and some other building materials were taken from Bromholm Priory, as some of the stones have a distinctly ecclesiastical flavour – in particular the small stone head over the top double door on the south-east side.

The long cattle sheds and square fodder room on this side are later additions. They

would have made two enclosed yards for over-wintering stock.

The barn is mainly brick, flint and thatch. The thatch would have been taken from the reed beds on the edge of the parish that belonged to the Hall estate. It is interesting that brick has been rendered to look like stone on some door frames. Stone was a prized and rare material in north Norfolk, and it all had to be shipped for long distances. Flints were the commonest building material and are used with great skill in the barn in long, even, graded rows.

The timber frames for the doors and roof of the barn were built on the ground and then hoisted into position. The door frames are original. The roof bosses are all numbered in Roman numerals. To save timber (even by 1581 timber of this size and quality was becoming scarce) hammer and tie beams alternate in the Paston roof. The effect is magnificent, and in some ways, because the whole structure is open to the view, it is as imposing as the church roofs of the medieval period. It is particularly interesting to compare this roof with the angel roof at Knapton church, a mile down the road.

The niches in the interior wall were for lamps. It is not known why Paston Great Barn is so tall – even taller than Waxham Barn. There are no signs of a gallery and the floor was sub-divided into stalls.

As recorded in *The Educated Pin*, an account of life in the village published in 1944 by Marjorie Mack, a descendant of the Pastons, the Barn was used not only for agricultural purposes but also for village gatherings. The last occasion was the dinner given by East Anglian Real Estate Properties for farm workers and families in 1976.

The barn is now owned by the North Norfolk Historic Buildings Trust and leased to Natural England, who have an interest in a colony of bats there. It is being fully restored – from what was a dangerous condition.

Bats!

As well as being a Scheduled Ancient Monument on account of its architectural and historical importance, Paston Great Barn is internationally important for its bat populations and has therefore been designated as a Special Area of Conservation (SAC) and Site of Special Scientific Interest (SSSI). More recently, it was declared a National Nature Reserve.

Seven species of bat have been recorded using the buildings, but it is on account of its population of Barbastelle bats that the barn is internationally important. Despite intensive research in recent years, the Barbastelle remains one of Britain's rarest and most enigmatic species of mammal.

The name Barbastelle is derived from the Latin *barba*, 'beard', and *stella*, 'star', referring to the fringe of pale hairs that protrudes from the bottom lip of the species. Their small eyes, rounded ears that join over the forehead and pug-like expression, resulting from their squat facial features, make them one of our most distinctive looking bats, giving them a permanently grumpy, 'just woken up' look.

The Barbastelle is rare and declining throughout most of its range.

When the maternity roost of Barbastelle bats was discovered at Paston Great Barn in 1998, it was the only such roost known in the whole of the UK. A handful of other roosts are now known in the UK, but the roost at Paston remains the only one known in a building.

The restoration of the Great Barn has involved major structural works. However, through careful planning and execution of the restoration programme the North Norfolk Historic Buildings Trust and Natural England have ensured the continued survival of the buildings whilst maintaining the maternity roost of Barbastelle bats which they support.

Access to the barn is by arrangement only. However, Natural England has teamed up with the Paston Heritage Society to provide guided tours of the barn during the winter months and bat walks during the summer.

Farms and Footpaths

Two farms in Paston show very clearly the contrasting farming methods that shaped the countryside in the 20th century. On the one hand there is Green Farm, owned by the Purdy family since 1820, and on the other is Hall Farm, the original Paston estate which was owned by East Anglian Real Estate Properties from the 1920s and is now in private hands.

FRANK GRAY AND OTHER MEN STANDING AT THE FORGE EARLY IN THE 20TH CENTURY

Green Farm and its footpaths have remained very much the same. The same field names and boundaries are used on today's estate map as were used 100 years ago. Hall Farm was used for 'factory farming'. All field boundaries have gone on the coastal side of the farm, and Hemp Lane and Craft Lane were ploughed up with them. Craft Lane has been restored as a footpath across the field and the Paston Way, a new footpath, remains open as a permissive path which runs from the old entrance to Craft Lane to Paston Heights. Hemp Lane is now only a 'grace and favour' right of way across a field for local residents. The entrance to Hemp Lane can be seen just beyond the Forge. Field Barn Loke ran to the south of the village when the land was bought for the Bacton gas site. This form of farming of course made it easier to use large machines on the land, but much of the individual character of the land was lost.

Villagers who remember the old paths have told me that the usual Sunday walk in the village was up Hemp Lane to the coast path, where the fathers would cut steps in the cliff each spring so that families could climb down to the beach. They would then return to the village by Craft Lane. The lanes were also used for farm purposes. There was a barn at the end of Hemp Lane, and horses, carts and wagons would go up there. Smaller children would be pushed in a pram, and driftwood and other flotsam would be brought up from the beach. Elizabeth Randell, whose father, Frank Gray, owned the builder's yard at the bottom of Hemp Lane, remembers playing in the lane and picking primroses and violets by the barn. The lane had high hedges and shady trees and was referred to as 'lovers' lane' by Clifford Burton. The lane was ploughed up when EARP bought Poplar Farm (now Dayspring) in 1965.

POPLAR FARM (NOW DAYSPRING)

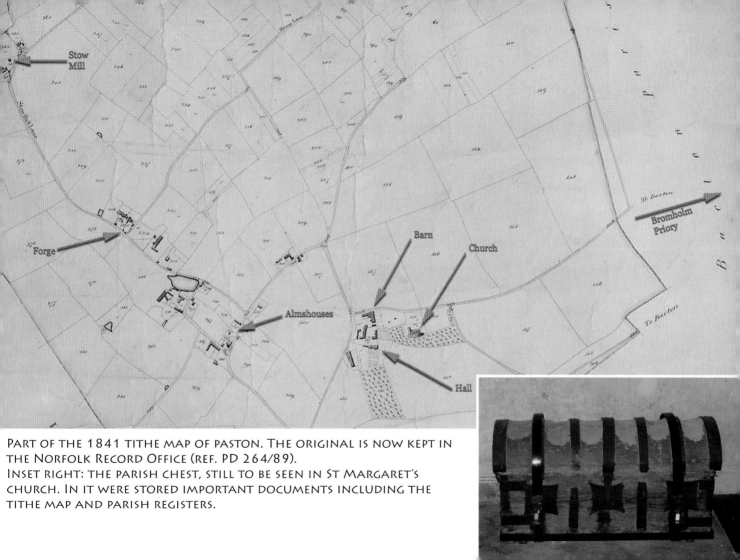

Stow
Mill

Forge

Barn

Church

Almshouses

Bromholm
Priory

To Bacton

Hall

PART OF THE 1841 TITHE MAP OF PASTON. THE ORIGINAL IS NOW KEPT IN
THE NORFOLK RECORD OFFICE (REF. PD 264/89).
INSET RIGHT: THE PARISH CHEST, STILL TO BE SEEN IN ST MARGARET'S
CHURCH. IN IT WERE STORED IMPORTANT DOCUMENTS INCLUDING THE
TITHE MAP AND PARISH REGISTERS.

North Walsham to Paston

Circular walk or cycle ride, 6½ miles (5½ miles to Pigney's Wood)

¶ From North Walsham take the Bacton Road (B1150) over Austen bridge and past the Old Wherry Inn. *This is where wherries used to turn on the North Walsham and Dilham canal; the Wherry Inn was the only Paston pub – rather a long way from the village!*

¶ Turn left after the bridge just before Rivermount house. On your left about quarter of a mile up the road is the car park for Pigney's Wood. Leave your car here and explore the wood – you can walk down to the old canal from here. *There is also a nature reserve to explore a little further up the road in* the old railway embankment.

¶ As an alternative route, it is possible to walk up the old railway line (the MGN line) to Knapton.

¶ From the car park, walk up the hill and turn right. The road is bisected by Green Lane – the oldest footpath in the village. This will take you up to Green Farm close by Paston and Knapton station

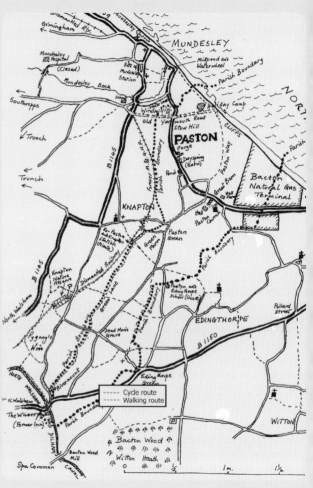

PASTON & KNAPTON STATION: AN OLD PHOTOGRAPH

– disused but still preserved by the present owners. If you are cycling, continue past the footpath to the crossroads known as Dead Man's Grave.

¶ Turn left and stay on the Quiet Lane until you reach Paston Green. From here it is a short walk into Paston on the Quiet Lanes network. To see the church you can turn sharp right after the entrance to Paston Hall. This new footpath will take you past the Great Barn and into the churchyard.

¶ Return to Paston Green and go through the railway bridge up into the village. *Knapton church's magnificent angel roof is well worth seeing so take a detour at this point into the church. Don't forget to look at the weathervane – designed by Cotman and therefore unique.*

¶ Leaving the church, go to the end of the village and turn left at the junction with the B1145. From here you re-enter the Quiet Lanes network and can walk past the old school and the nature reserve and back to Pigney's Wood.

As you will see from the map, the Quiet Lanes network is criss-crossed with footpaths, all of which form pleasant alternative routes if you are exploring on horseback or on foot – they do not lend themselves to cycling!

Paston & Edingthorpe School

A School Board for the united parishes of Paston and Edingthorpe was formed in 1875. The Board School was erected in 1878 on the parish boundary of the two villages. Intended to house 100 children, it had an average attendance that never exceeded 70. When the school closed in 1959 numbers had fallen to 22, and they were transferred to Bacton. Among those who attended a party to mark the closure of the school was Mrs Alice Pardon of Pond Cottage, Paston, who was one of the first pupils. Her father had helped to build the school. She recalled that she had received her schooling in a cottage in the village before the Board School was built.

The school is now a private residence but the Honours Board has been preserved and hangs in Edingthorpe Parish Church.

THE LAST PUPILS OF THE VILLAGE SCHOOL, PHOTOGRAPHED IN 1959

Paston and Bromholm

About 6 miles (circular walk)

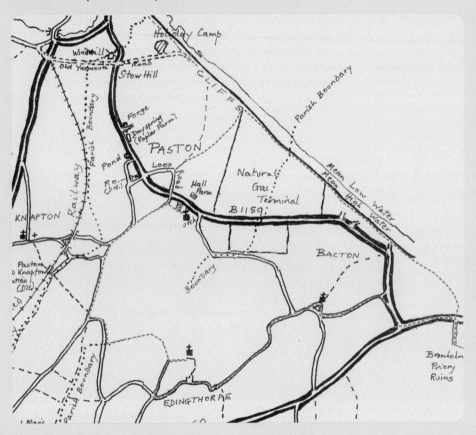

This walk can be started either from the public car park in Abbey Street, Bacton, or the Great Barn car park on the coast road at Paston. It is described here from Paston.

¶ Go into the churchyard and take the footpath to the right that runs behind the Great Barn. *This is also the best viewing point for the Great Barn.*

¶ At the end of the path, turn left down the Quiet Lane and follow it to Paston Green (about a quarter of a mile). *Paston Green was one of the three parts of Paston parish and was also a Paston manor – Green Farm still remains here, and the land is farmed by the same family who bought it from the Ketton Cremers, who bought it from the Ansons. It is farmed by organic methods, and the hedges bear witness to the diversity of plant life left to riot unchanged over the centuries. It is in marked contrast to the Hall Farm lands to the north of the church, which were devastated when turned into one enormous field in the 1960s, destroying hedges and footpaths in the process. The current owners of Hall Farm are trying to redress the balance. The quiet lanes between Paston and Bacton have a large variety of plants and, in consequence, wildlife. It is possible to see foxes, owls, deer, hares and, of course, rabbits commonly – and weasels, stoats and bats less frequently.*

¶ From Paston Green, continue up the hill and then down towards North Walsham, but turn left at the bottom, at the junction signposted Edingthorpe. Where the road turns right, take the footpath that runs parallel to the road and then turns left as it approaches the old Paston and Edingthorpe school. *The school may be viewed a few yards further on: it was placed on the boundary of the two villages with the playground in both parishes to avoid rivalries. This is quite common in North Norfolk but very inconvenient for the pupils, as the schools were often at some distance from either village!*

¶ Follow the footpath, with Edingthorpe cthurch directly ahead. Where a metalled road joins it from right (and stops) continue up the hillside track to the church – *a beautiful gem of a building in a lovely spot.*

¶ From the church, return down the track, turn left down the metalled road and at the crossroads turn left towards Bacton, eventually reaching Bacton church, which can be accessed up a short paved track to the left.

¶ From Bacton church, take the Quiet Lane down to the village, taking the right fork by a pond, and turn right along the coast road. At the junction with the B1159 turn left into the village and past the school. Cross the

road at the layby and turn into Abbey Street. *You will see the Abbey gateway ahead of you. From this viewpoint it is possible to see how grand Bromholm Priory was, as many of the older houses were owned by the priory and have survived the Reformation. At the gateway you can get closer to the ruins by taking the public footpath on your left and peering through holes in the hedge or, if you make an appointment with the tenants or owner of Abbey Farm, it may be possible to see them from the farmyard. Bromholm Priory is an ancient scheduled monument in the care of Natural England/English Heritage and was placed on the 'at risk' register in 2008. Public interest in the ruins is growing, but they have never been excavated, and a tantalising amount of English history lies close to the surface below Bacton. Hopefully, the story of the Paston family will alert public attention to the importance of these ruins before they disappear completely.*

¶ From the Priory, it is pleasant to cross the road and take the stony lane opposite which curves to the right and goes down to the sea. From here at low tide you can walk along the beach to Cable Gap and then take the cliff path to Paston, going up the hill past the gas site. At the end of the gas site fence turn left across the field (Craft Lane)

THE PRECARIOUS RUINS OF BROM-HOLM PRIORY IN FIELDS AT BACTON.

and join Paston Way just above the junction with the Loop road. Turn left down the Loop road and cross at the junction back to the footpath to the church around the back of Paston Great Barn.

Bromholm Priory

In 1113 William de Glanville, cousin to the first Pastons and the man who granted the land for Paston, founded Bromholm Priory at Bacton. It was a cell for seven or eight Cluniac monks from Castle Acre.

The original building was small, but a

considerable enlargement took place in the early 13th century. Probably to replace the smaller buildings, a chapter house and dormitory were built. This expansion was due to the Priory's wardship of a 'valuable relic'.

Baldwin, Count of Flanders and Emperor of Constantinople, was continually harassed by infidel kings. Before marching into battle against his enemies, he always paraded 'the Cross of our Lord' and other relics in front of the foe. On the last occasion he neglected this ritual, and he and many of his followers died.

Baldwin's chaplain, who was of English extraction, left Constantinople with his clerics, plus 'the Cross of our Lord' and other relics. On arrival in England he went to St Albans and sold an ornamented cross, two fingers of St Margaret and some other relics to a monk there. He also showed the monk what he claimed was a piece of the true cross. The monk didn't believe him, and the chaplain left.

Many monasteries later he came to the Chapel of Bromholm, which was poor. The prior and brethren were overjoyed to receive

such a treasure and carried the cross into the oratory and preserved it there. The 'Cross of our Lord' brought prosperity to Bromholm on its arrival in 1223. Soon afterwards miracles began to occur. According to Capgrave, 19 blind men had their sight restored, and 39 men were raised from the dead. Such miracles brought fame, and Bromholm became a focus for pilgrims.

In 1233 Henry III and his court stayed at Bromholm and conferred several grants on the monastery. By 1298 Bromholm had become prosperous, and so Pope Celestine V absolved Bromholm of its subjection to Castle Acre.

At the dissolution of the monasteries, the Priory was granted to Sir Thomas Wodehouse of Waxham. The Paston family were also patrons of the Priory. Sir John Paston, on his death in 1466, was brought from London to Bromholm to be buried amid much pomp and ceremony.

Extensive remains still stand, although they are now used as a farm storage area. The church was originally 200 feet (60m) long, 50 feet (15m) wide, with transepts 90 feet (27m) across. There are also rumoured to be the remains of a secret tunnel linking the priory with St Margaret's church, complete with golden gates.

BROMHOLM PRIORY RUINS: LITHO-GRAPH BY J. COTMAN. LEFT: PLAN OF THE PRIORY BUILDINGS.

A Funeral Feast

In 1466 John Paston died in London. His body was brought to Bromholm for interment, resting one night at St Peter Hungate, Norwich, on the way. This passage is from Blomefield's account of the funeral (in volume 6 of his *History of Norfolk*):

For three continuous days one man was engaged in no other occupation than that of flaying beasts, and provision was made of 13 barrels of beer, 27 barrels of ale, one barrel of beer of the greatest assyze and a runlet of red wine of 15 gallons. All these, however copious they may seem, proved inadequate to the demand: for the account goes on to state that five coombs of malt at one time and ten at another were brewed up expressly for the occasion. Meat too was in proportion to the liquor; the county round about must have been swept of geese, chickens, capouns and such small gear, all which – with the 1300 eggs, 20 gallons of milk and eight of cream, and the 41 pig, 49 calves and 10 'nete' slain and devoured – gives a fearful picture of the scene of festivity the abbey walls at the time beheld. Amongst such provisions the article of bread bears nearly the same proportion as in Falstaff's bill of fare. The one halfpenny-worth of the staff of life to the inordinate quantity of sack was acted over again in Bromholm Priory; but then, on the other hand, in the matter of consumption, the torches, the many pounds' weight of wax to burn over the grave and the separate candle of enormous stature and girth, form prodigious items. No less then £20 was changed from gold into smaller coin that it might be showered amongst the attendant throng and 26 marks in copper had been used for the same object in London before the procession begun to move. A barber was occupied five days in smartening up the monks for the ceremony; and the 'reke of the torches at the dirge' was so great that the glazier had to remove two panes to permit the fumes to escape.

John Paston's tomb was moved to the east end of Paston church after the dissolution of the monasteries in 1536.

Caister Castle and Mautby

Mautby was the home of Margaret Paston's family. She was an only child and heir to her father's lands – which, of course, is why she was such a desirable match for young John Paston. In her will she asked to be buried in the south aisle of Mautby church, with her ancestors, but that aisle of the church was badly neglected and fell down in the 17th or 18th century. It is possible (just) to see the tomb of the last of her Mauteby ancestors, a knight templar, circa 1250, in the chancel, partly concealed by the pews.

Mautby church is a well preserved, thatched, round tower church. Mautby itself dates back to before the Domesday book, when there was a village, mill and seven salt works (the sea was closer then). By 1199 the Lordship had passed to the de Mauteby family who held it until James I. The churchyard is peaceful and well kept, and a very pleasant place to remember how Norfolk once was. It is no longer possible to walk directly to Caister castle by footpath but it is worth walking to the edge of the marshes to try and imagine this place when Margaret lived here and the coast was empty towards Yarmouth.

It is possible to see the tower at Caister, still dominating the local skyline – when it was new, what a symbol of defiance to build, four tall towers looking out over the dangerous North Sea!

Margaret is one of the characters that appear most strongly in the letters. She writes forcefully and well and, while we may speculate that she sought peace at Mautby in death because she found little in her marriage to John Paston, she faithfully aligned herself with his family through all the troubles recorded in the letters. It is probably to her that we owe the preservation of the letters – was it because she married into a family of lawyers that she destroyed so little, not even the letters that end 'burn this as soon as you have read it'? Or did she acquire the habit from Agnes, her mother-in-law?

She, representing her husband, fought long and hard for the Paston property; when carried out from Gresham by Lord Moleyns' men, she merely seeks refuge nearby. Besieged at Caister, she writes to her second son to come quickly but also demands more weapons and food rather than an opportunity to concede

defeat. She was responsible for her household and her children and all the men and women who served them. She writes of medicines that may help, relays news and takes active part in chivvying her men to fight.

Here she writes to her husband, John, who is sick in London (1443):

I entreat you with all my heart to undertake to send me a letter as quickly as possible, if writing is no trouble to you, and that you undertake to send me word how your illness is. If I might have had my way I would have seen you before now. I would rather you were at home, if your comfort and illness could be as well looked after here as it is where you are now, than have a new gown, even if it were of scarlet.

She was proud of her Mautby ancestors (much more distinguished than the newcomers to aristocratic Norfolk, the Pastons). It was through Margaret's family connections that John became lawyer to their richer neighbour, Sir John Fastolf of Caister castle.

Sir John built the castle between 1432 and 1446. It is one of the earliest large brick buildings in England. (Of course, in Norfolk, stone was hard to come by.) It is rectangular with the inner moat still existing most of the way around. One of the four towers

CAISTER CASTLE TODAY. INSET: A POSTCARD DATING
FROM 1905, COLOURED BY SOMEONE WHO DIDN'T
KNOW THAT THIS CASTLE WAS MADE OF RED BRICK!

still remains, 90 feet (27m) high, and can be climbed for an excellent view of the surrounding countryside. It was built to be defensible from land and sea. No windows face outwards over the moat at ground floor level. The only time it was defended, by her son John Paston the younger in 1469, it stood up well to siege. With only a small garrison, they managed to hold it for three weeks against the Duke of Norfolk's troops, a far larger and more powerful company. The siege was settled by agreement: although the castle could be held at cost of lives and weaponry to both sides, a favourable agreement was the preferred way to settle disputes in the 15th century. Their ideas on honour and warfare are strange to us, but serving alternately on different sides of a dispute was common in these times. To the Paston family, and to families like them, squashed between the mighty lords of England and the commons, an ability to be flexible and to use a judicious mixture of flattery, hard work and application in the law courts was exceedingly important if a family was to survive. There was no animosity in their fighting – it was a question of property. As John Paston II says to Margaret, 'By my troth, I would rather lose the manor of Caister than the life of the simplest man therein, if that may save him.' Even more, the ultimate loyalty and duty of the members of the family was to the family itself and their dependants. With their rise in status came a rise in duties to those who served and to those they served – ultimately the King.

Caister Castle

Margaret Paston to John Paston II, 12th September 1469

I greet you well, letting you know that your brother and his fellowship stand in great jeopardy at Caister . . . Daubney and Berney are dead and others badly hurt, and gunpowder and arrows are lacking. The place is badly broken down by the guns of the other party, so that unless they have hasty help, they are likely to lose both their lives and the place, which will be the greatest rebuke to you that ever came to any gentleman. For every man in this country marvels greatly

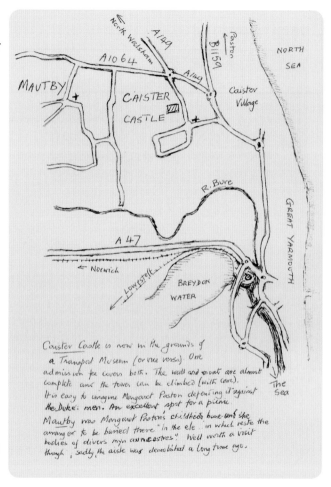

Caister Castle is now in the grounds of a Transport Museum (or vice versa). One admission fee covers both. The wall and moat are almost complete and the tower can be climbed (with care). It is easy to imagine Margaret Paston defending it against the Duke's men. An excellent spot for a picnic. Mautby was Margaret Paston's childhood home and she arranged to be buried there "In the ele . in which reste the bodies of divers myn auncestres". Well worth a visit though, sadly the aisle was demolished a long time ago.

that you suffer them to be for so long in great jeopardy without help or other remedy.

John Paston II to Margaret Paston, 15th September 1469

Mother, on Saturday last, both Daubney and Berney were alive and merry, and I suppose that there has come no man out of that place since who could have informed you of their deaths. And as for the fierceness of the Duke and his people . . . I am sure that it was agreed . . . that a truce and abstinence from war should endure until Monday next, and then I think that a truce will be made for another week, by which time I hope that a good conclusion will be found . . . But Mother, I feel by your writing that you think I will not do my duty unless you send me heavy tidings; but if I needed a letter to wake me up at this time, I would indeed be a sluggish fellow. I assure you that I have heard ten times worse tidings since the siege began than any letter that you wrote me, and . . . this I can assure you, that those within have no worse rest than I have, nor fear more danger.

Margaret Paston to John Paston II, 22nd/30th September 1469

It appears from the letter you sent me . . . that you think that I am writing to you fables and imaginings, but I do not do so. I have written as

I have been informed, and I will continue to do so. It was reported to me that both Daubney and Berney were dead, but for certain Daubney is dead, God rest his soul . . . And as for the yielding of Caister . . . I would that this had been done before this time and then there would not have been so much harm done as there has been in various ways. For many of our well-wishers are put to loss for our sake.

From John Paston III

Right worshipful sir, I recommend me to you. And as for the surrender of Caister, John Chapman can tell you as well as myself how we were forced to it. As for John Chapman and his fellows, I have provided that each of them be paid 40 shillings, and together with the money they had of you and Daubney, that is enough for the time that they have done you service. I pray you give them thanks, for by my troth they have as well deserved it as any men that ever lived . . . Writtle promised to send you the details of the surrender agreement. We were sore lacking in victuals, gunpowder and men's hearts, and lack of certainty of rescue drove us to the treaty.

John Paston II spent the next 11 years trying to get the manor of Caister back both in the law courts and by serving faithfully on the battlefield. At the Battle of Barnet in 1471,

both brothers were involved in pitched battle; John sounds suitably exited as he writes to their mother:

Blessed be God, my brother John is alive and fares well and is in no peril of death. Nevertheless he is hurt with an arrow in his right arm beneath the elbow. I have sent him a surgeon who has dressed it.

The Duke of Norfolk died in January 1476, and John Paston II hastily moved to reoccupy Caister castle:

23rd January 1476

I ensure you your sending to Caister is evil taken among my lord's folks, insomuch that some say you tendered little my lord's death inasmuch as you would so soon enter his property on his decease . . . It is thought here by such as be your friends in my lord's house that, if my lady have once the grant of wardship of her child, that she will occupy Caister with other lands, and lay the default of your unkind hastiness of entry without her assent. Wherefore in any wise, get you a patent from the King sealed before hers, by any means possible . . .

The King granted the patent and the Duchess of Norfolk gave up her dead husband's claim.

Gresham, Baconsthorpe & Barningham Winter

This triangle of houses connected with the Paston family can be explored on foot or by car.

It is easiest to start at Baconsthorpe castle. Now a moated ruin in the care of English Heritage, it was at the time of the Paston letters in the keeping of the Heydon family. John Heydon stood against John Paston in a trial to prove that he was not a free man by ancestry and could not therefore hold Caister Castle, so he was certainly no friend to the Pastons. Yet within a generation the Pastons had succeeded in becoming one of the four most powerful families in Norfolk, William Paston in 1500 marrying Bridget Heydon, John's granddaughter.

The layout and design of Baconsthorpe clearly shows the transition from moated and defensible dwelling to gentleman's country house. When the castle was built, around 1460, its moat and drawbridge were needed and the three-storey inner gatehouse provided ample, defensible room for the entire household. Whereas Caister was allowed to fall into decay, Baconsthorpe Castle was transformed with the addition of the outer gatehouse as a rather grander dwelling, and the inner dwelling within the walls of the original castle was used as a wool factory with the north tower becoming a fullers pit. The castle was inhabited until the Civil War.

The castle is maintained by English Heritage but it is unstaffed and free. The beautiful ruins are excellent for picnics and imaginative play,

Moat

Lake

Gatehouse

Hall

Moat

Gatehouse

P

Farm

but please keep children off the walls. The approach is through a working farm.

It is a short drive from here to Barningham and Gresham – or it is possible to cycle or walk.

Gresham

Gresham, by contrast, is a deserted ruin. The castle from which Margaret Paston was carried by Lord Moleyns' men has never been restored but sits secretly within the moat covered with brambles and ivy – although there are signs of tunnelling through the undergrowth and across the moat to the ruins. Only the footings of the castle remain. Robert Hungerford, Lord Moleyns, assumed he had the right to take the castle from the Pastons because, at the time, the greatest lords of the land including the Duke of Norfolk were outraged by John Paston's inheritance of Caister Castle from Fastolf. Lord Moleyns' father had sold the castle (well, half of it) to William Paston who passed it on to his son John in his will, but Lord Moleyns besieged it on the 28th January 1449 with 1,000 men at arms (most of them from Wiltshire, his principal seat, so they had no local loyalties). Margaret sat inside it in the dark winter night with her chaplain,

THE SITE OF GRESHAM CASTLE IS NOW JUST AN OVERGROWN MOATED RUIN –
YOU CAN GET ACROSS THE MOAT (PICTURE INSET) BUT THIS IS ALL PRIVATE PROPERTY.

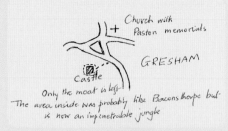

Church with Paston memorials

GRESHAM

Castle

Only the moat is left. The area inside was probably like Baconsthorpe but is now an impenetrable jungle

Friar Brackley, and 12 serving men. John was in London again, trying to prove title to his property in the courts. John Paston describes events in this petition to Parliament in 1449.

The said Lord Moleyns sent to the said mansion a riotous people to the number of a thousand persons . . . arrayed in manner of war, with cuirasses, briganders and jacks [a type of body armour], sallets, bows, guns, pans with fire, long crooks to drag down houses . . . and long trees with which they broke up the gates and doors, and so came into the mansion, the wife of your beseecher at that time being therin, and twelve persons with her. The which twelve persons they drove out of said mansion and mined down the wall of the chamber wherein the wife of your beseecher was, and bore her out of the gates; and cut asunder the posts of the houses and let them fall and broke up all the chambers and coffers within the said mansion and rifled . . . and bore away all the stuff to the value of £200.

Even allowing for some exaggeration, it must have been a terrifying experience for Margaret. She took refuge with a friend, John Damme at Sustead. John Winter of Barningham Winter was a supporter of Moleyns. It seems the countryside took sides in the Pastons' quarrels and often, at this time, against John Paston. At this stage it was not evident that the Paston family would succeed in their social climbing. Actually the whole Paston story of this time beggars belief. That this man, without noble ancestors and without any claims to aptitude at fighting, should hold his lands and increase them in this century of unrest, simply by repeated petitioning of the King and parliament to uphold the law of the country rather than the might of the aristocracy against lesser men, is remarkable. And Margaret was a remarkable woman in her unflinching support of John.

If you wander up to the church at Gresham, however, it is clear that the Paston family were not driven out, despite the destruction of the castle. They regained their right to the property in October but never rebuilt the castle. It was much older than their other properties: the licence to crenellate Gresham castle is dated 1318. With such

THE VILLAGE SIGN AT GRESHAM SHOWS THE PASTONS' ARMS AS WELL AS THE CASTLE.

notable dwellings as the newly built Caister castle and Oxburgh and nearby Baconsthorpe being built at the time, perhaps it seemed unfashionable. They continued to collect the rents and farm the land, however. Look at the board of incumbents presented to the parish: for two hundred years after the castle was invaded by Lord Moleyns, the patrons are still the Paston family.

Barningham Winter

From Gresham it is a short distance to Barningham Winter and one can imagine an angry Margaret with her servants riding briskly down the tracks towards nearby Sustead. Barningham Hall is open to the public on rare occasions but the unusual and beautiful little church can be reached by driving or walking through the park gates.

It is easy to see why Margaret was so afraid in 1449. Eleanor, daughter of Edmund Winter of Barningham Winter, married John Heydon of Baconsthorpe around 1450, and Heydon

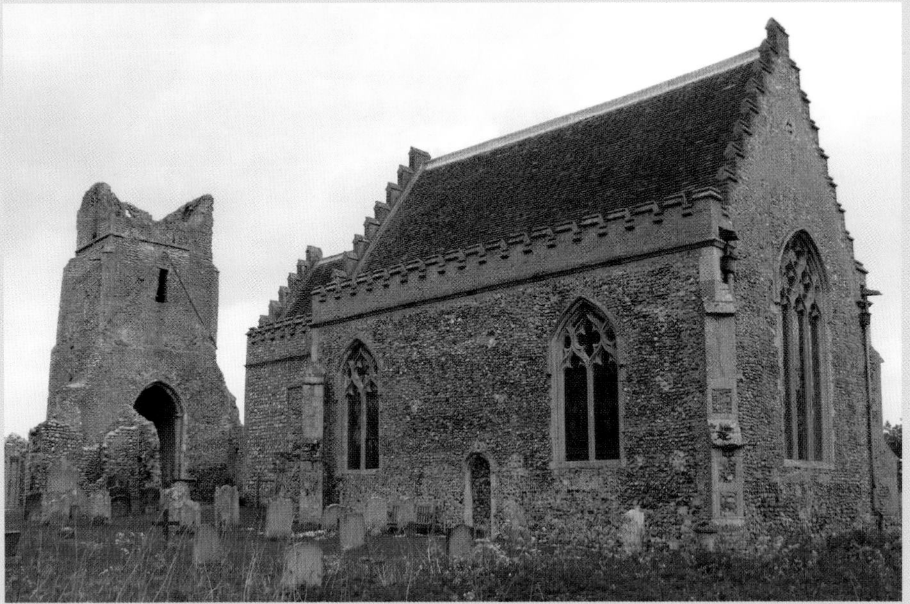

Barningham Winter church. The nave was demolished centuries ago, leaving the ruined tower and the restored chancel with an 1830 extension (with lower roof line) accommodating a gallery.

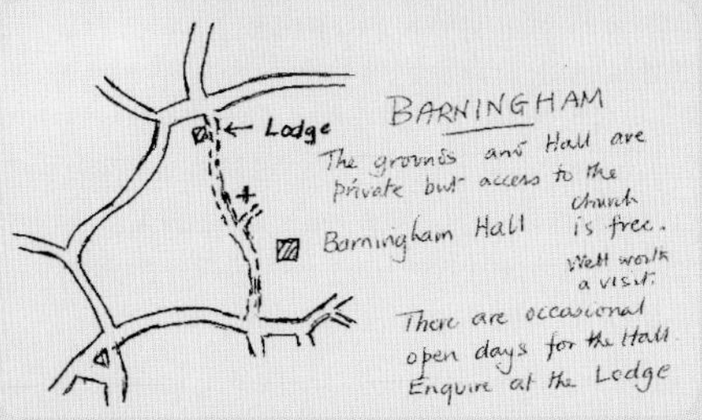
BARNINGHAM
Lodge
The grounds and Hall are private but access to the church is free.
Barningham Hall
Well worth a visit.
There are occasional open days for the Hall. Enquire at the Lodge

had opposed the Paston family from the start. In 1451, Margaret writes to John that

It is said here that the King will come to this country and that Sir Thomas Tuddenham and Heydon are well cherished with him. And also it is said that they shall have as great a rule in this country as ever they had, and many more folks are sorry therefore than merry . . . The boasting is so great on the other party that it makes the tenants sore afraid that you will not enjoy [Gresham manor].

In Edmund Winter's will, dated 20th February 1447, he gives Alice, his wife, the manor of Barningham for life, remainder to John his son. He was buried in Barningham church, before the high altar.

He is mentioned as a member of the Guild of St George in Norwich. In 1468 an inventory was made of all the goods, jewels etc belonging to the guild, one of which was 'a precious relique amongst other holy relicks' in the cathedral church of the Blessed Trinity at Norwich 'that is to sey, one Angell silver and guylt bering the arms of Seynt George, ye which was given to the seid fraternite by John Fastolf, Knight'. Members of this guild included Sir Brian Stapleton, Sir John Fastolf, Lord William de la Pole, earl of Suffolk, Lord Bardolf, William Paston, the King's Chief Justice (John's father), Sir John Hevenyngham, Edmund Winter and John Heydon. Perhaps membership of the guild and the ties of pride in Norfolk enabled the Pastons to marry into families with whom they appear to have been frequently at loggerheads.

Barningham Winter, too, became a Paston property and the Hall was rebuilt by Edward Paston in 1612. It is a fine example of Jacobean architecture. The landscaped grounds (and the south front of the house) are the work of Humphry Repton and John Adey Repton. It is the only great house built by the Pastons still standing and not ruined but, of course, its building reflects the status

of the Pastons not in the period of the letters but in later years when they were one of the four great families of Norfolk. The church was rebuilt in Georgian style and is charming. At the East end of the church is a poignant stone tablet to a small John Paston who died just before his first birthday in 1729:

He just stop'd here below
On his Journey to Above,
And felt the Agonies of Expiring nature
to heighten his Relish of the Joys of Heaven.

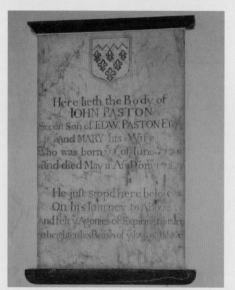

The squabbling gentry of 15th-century north Norfolk rebuilt their homes in the 16th and 17th centuries because so much of the medieval way of life changed so quickly with the advent of the Tudors. At the Battle of Bosworth, John Paston supplied liveried men to support John Howard, Duke of Norfolk. But Henry Tudor changed the protocol for battles after Bosworth by his laws against livery and maintenance; the rival private armies of the great lords of England became a thing of the past. Henry even declared those who fought against him at Bosworth and for Richard II to be traitors – definitely not cricket in terms of warfare before this date, as the Pastons' numerous changes of allegiance show. The Tudors brought peace to war torn England and houses reflected the prosperity that resulted for those who served the king. And then came the Reformation.

We tend to despise families like the Pastons that maintained loyalty to their own interests above all principles. We forget that loyalty at this time was to the Lord's anointed, the King, who was, above all, ruling England by the grace of Almighty God. Whatever one's personal feelings, there was no other choice than to support the King or to be a traitor. The Civil War changed all that.

The Paston Household

As a young woman, Margaret Paston would have learnt general household skills at her mother's side. Girls learnt all they needed by being their mother's extra hands. Margaret had wealthy relations and inherited her father's estate; her husband John was a well educated man, perhaps a Yeoman of the stables to the King (Henry VII) in 1438–9. A lawyer who spent much of his time in London, he became a trusted councillor to Sir John Fastolf and main heir to his property. He was a JP for Norfolk from November 1460 and an MP for Norfolk in 1460–61.

Young men such as John Paston were often sent away to be brought up and educated in someone else's household acting as a page, then squire – a little like modern upper class families sending their children to boarding school. This way they learnt how to manage a large household, to mix in high society and to make suitable friends and allies for future needs. Girls, a pawn until they married to their father's advantage, were then the husband's chattel, but John did well in his choice of wife as Margaret brought wealth, lands and housewifely skills into their

marriage. She also learnt more under the wings of Agnes, her mother-in-law, a very formidable lady who, when widowed in 1444, spent her first years at Paston and Norwich then later with her son William in London.

Medieval society was highly structured with each person knowing their place – hence the furore when John and Margaret's daughter Margery was clandestinely married to Richard Calle, a servant, in 1469. A high class wealthy family would have a retinue for which John and Margaret had full responsibility. At Caister it would probably consist of:

The **Chief Steward** who had to 'superintend the household and ensure their livery be clean and neat and comely worn and that their shoes be good. He had to keep account of the alms that it be not wasted on tips to boys and knaves about the Hall or spent on supper dainties for grooms. He is to make his household dine together in Hall sitting in fellowship.'

The **Clerk,** often a monk, who kept the account rolls and records. His underlings weighed and checked, counted and

overlooked the rent payment of goods and works.

The **Marshall,** who was expected to present guests, messengers or important matters to his Lord and relay orders to the other servants.

The **Usher of the House** was responsible for the daily running of the household. Under his charge was the **Groom of the Hall** whose main responsibility was the supervision of the cleaning.

The **Pages of the Hall** dealt with putting up and removing meal tables, straw for sleepers at night, clearing of rushes, fetching of fresh boughs to fill the torch rings in summer and stopping dog fights at meal times.

The **Groom of the Fire** attended to fuel supplies for torches and flambeaux. Under him were the **Pages Fire and Torches** who carried torches, lit bedroom fires and gave out candles to squires (with extra good ones for the Clerk and Doctor).

The **Pages of the Door** ran messages such as fetching alms from the clerk to pay beggars.

The **Grooms of the Chamber** had charge of the bedrooms, making up the twisted straw pallets for the beds, taking charge of the women who supplied and mended the linen, and bringing in the bath and washing water. Once the Master had risen and gone to Mass they would turn the bedroom into a day sitting room.

The **Groom of the Wardrobe** was a valet to the Lord, attending to his clothes, helping him to dress and bringing him a drink. He would set the nightlight in a bowl of water and turn away the cats and dogs from the bedroom.

Other household servants included the **Groom of the Stable**, the **Groom of Water** and the **Butler**. All these people had to be fed, so there were cooks, maids and skivvies plus people who worked in the garden, the understaff and the nursery staff who looked after the children of the family.

This was a huge responsibility for Margaret, whose husband John was often away in London – even at one time in the debtors'

prison. She had to endure raids on her home and lands by the troops of the Duke of Norfolk and cope with every eventuality. She was a wife, mother, nurse/healer, gardener, organiser and general factotum. She was an intelligent, strong and very level headed lady who dictated and received a large number of the Paston Letters. Thanks to her thriftiness in never throwing anything out, we know more about Paston lives from a personal perspective than is usually discovered.

The Pastons' Norwich

Just under 3 miles (circular walk)

The Pastons would recognise bits of Norwich, be horrified by changes and be amazed by the juxtaposition of several centuries' inventions and styles jostling for a spot in their once familiar city.

They had a house in Princes Street, mentioned by John Paston III in 1469 (originally Margaret's house). John Paston III bought a house in King Street which had been built for a rich and famous Jew of the Jurnet family and is now known as the Music House. The fifteenth century undercroft and south range of that building on the river were probably added when John Paston II owned the house. It is possible to visit the Paston Room there still, as it is now part of Wensum Lodge, an adult education centre.

This walk starts at the back of Blackfriars monastery, a Benedictine foundation and now part arts college and part public facility for concerts and other functions, such as beer festivals and collectors' fairs.

St Andrews and Blackfriars Halls in Norwich are the most complete friary complex

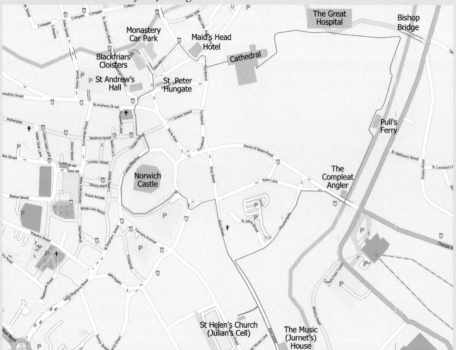

BLACKFRIARS CLOISTERS

surviving in this country and have been welcoming visitors since they passed into civic hands in 1538.

The friary church, dedicated to St John the Baptist and the largest of the four city friaries, was begun in 1326 but not finished until 1470 because a fire destroyed most of the building in 1413. Five original windows in St Andrews Hall and the great east window in Blackfriars were incorporated into the new building. The roof-beams for Blackfriars and the hammer-beams in St Andrews roof were the gift of the Paston family, together with the superb 15th-century doors, bearing the arms of Paston and Mautby, in the south porch.

¶ To reach the parking area, turn off Tombland opposite the cathedral and into Princes Street. Turn right at the top of Elm Hill by St Peter Hungate and continue down towards the river to the Monastery park, going straight on where Elm Hill bends right.

¶ Take a moment to explore the cloisters at the bottom of the car park. Leave the top of the car park and turn left into Elm Hill. *Facing the back of Blackfriars is The Britons Arms, which housed a religious community of women and is the only building on Elm Hill to have come through a great fire of*

ELM HILL. THE HOUSE ON THE RIGHT WAS ONCE THOUGHT TO HAVE BELONGED TO THE PASTONS.

1507, which burned for four days. The houses were rebuilt soon after, but by the nineteenth century they had become slums and were in danger of demolition. The Norwich Society was formed in the 1920s and was instrumental in ensuring their restoration.

Moving down Elm Hill, you will find on the left at 22–24 The Strangers' Club, a building dating from the early 16th century and once alleged to have belonged to the Paston family. The River Wensum flows some yards behind the houses on this side.

On the right, next to Norris Court Gardens, at 41–43, is Pettus House, restored in 1948–49. It was, as Pevsner writes, 'a town house of the Pastons, the original having been a large courtyard house extending over all of Wrights Court to the SE of St Simon and St Jude. The present house was rebuilt by Augustine Steward after the 1507 fire.'

¶ At the bottom of Elm Hill, turn right towards the cathedral. Cross the road by the Maid's Head hotel, which dates back to the 13th century, and enter the cathedral precincts by the Erpingham Gate. Go straight ahead and enter by the west door.

William Paston, the good judge, and his wife Agnes Berry are buried here. It was William's father Clement's decision to send his son to be educated that built the family fortunes. There was no school recorded near Paston, and the cathedral school was certainly in existence at this time. It was founded in 1413. Was William educated here? If you are lucky, it is possible still

*to hear the boys of the 'singing school'
practising close by the cathedral, just as
in the Pastons' time. Norwich is one of the
cathedrals where the past of the building is
still discernible, and the unity of faith and
worship in the same place for so long seems
more important than the changes of liturgy
and creed. This is not a place where change
came easily, however.*

¶ Leave the cathedral by the south transept
door and turn east (left) down a wide,
winding path to the lesser known exit to
Bishopgate which takes you past the Great
Hospital to Bishop Bridge. *Here the Lollards
were walked to the Lollards' Pit to be burnt
alive. John Foxe's Acts and Monuments,
popularly known as Foxe's Book of Martyrs,
tells many of their stories – although with
a strong anti-Catholic bias. Thus we learn
of William White, a priest from Kent who
moved to Ludham to preach dissent. Along
with fellow Lollards Hugh Pye and John
Waddon, White was executed in September
1428 in a space off Riverside Road close to
where the gasholder now stands, opposite
Bishop Bridge, and it was given the name
Lollards' Pit. The last stand of the Lollards in
1381 was at North Walsham – the Pastons
would certainly know of the 'heresy', but
they were not known to comment on*

religious beliefs other than their own.

¶ Turn right along the lovely riverside path
just before Bishop Bridge, and you will come
to Pull's Ferry. *This building dates to the
15th century, when Norwich was an inland
port thriving through trade with the Low*

*Countries. Worsted cloth from Norfolk was
shipped in single-masted craft called keels
or wherries along the Wensum and Yare to
Yarmouth and then in seagoing vessels to
Europe, with luxury goods such as wine and
spices coming back in exchange. They were
unloaded at private staithes and stored in
riverside warehouses.*

¶ Keep on the riverside path until it
emerges through the Compleat Angler pub's
courtyard on to Prince of Wales Road. Cross
the road towards the Nelson hotel, opposite
Norwich station. Turn right up Prince of
Wales Road and keep to the left where the
road forks. Turn left at the traffic lights and
walk up Mountergate to the top. Turn left
down King Street. *This is an area under
development at the time of writing, and King
Street itself – once the main north–south
route through Norwich – is a mixture of
restored old properties, tastefully designed
new ones and some that badly need
attention or, in some cases, demolition.*

*Many wealthy local families, including the
Pastons and the Heydons, had town houses
in King Street. The Pastons' house is now
known as the Music House and is part of
Wensum Lodge. Before you reach that, however, you come to the Dragon Hall. This has
been lived in since Saxon times, but came
to prominence in the later medieval period.
Robert Toppes was a cloth merchant with
interests throughout Norfolk. Four times
Mayor of Norwich in the mid-15th century,
his King Street property was a showroom for
his top-class continental goods. The building gets its name from a decorative carving
found in the roof of the building when it
was studied by archaeologists. This may
reflect membership of the trade guild of St
George, which was popular from the 14th*

century on. William Paston (the good judge) was a member. On the Feast of St George a procession would go through King Street to Tombland with Snap, a colourful hobby-horse with dragon wings and snappable jaws, at its head. Snap remains the city's symbol, and the regalia can be seen in the Castle Museum.

¶ After visiting the Music House, about 100 yards further on, retrace your steps along King Street (possibly taking a slight diversion up St Julian's Alley to view the world-famous shrine of Mother Julian), pass the junction with Mountergate and at the traffic lights turn left and walk up towards the castle. This is most easily accessed by crossing Cattle Market Street and walking

across the entrance to the Castle Mall car park, then left through a gate onto a wide, delightful path that passes in front of an open-air theatre. Fifty yards (45m) further along you can walk up steps to the left and reach the castle entrance across a high bridge: there is also a lift on the right of the path, but it is not always working. *If you have time and money, explore the interior of the Castle – hopefully the poignant painting The Pastons' Treasure will be on display, together with some remnants of the treasures of Oxnead Hall.*

The Castle mound is a good place to get a view of the roads of medieval Norwich, with the Castle and the Cathedral spire dominating the spiralling streets marked by the many churches of Norwich.

¶ From the Castle mound go back down and turn right out on to Castle Meadow.

THE PASTON HOUSE IN KING STREET, NORWICH – 'THE MUSIC HOUSE'

Cross the road and continue to the right till you reach Opie Street. Turn left, then after 50 yards (45m) turn left and right to cross the pedestrianised London Street and continue down St Andrews Hill to St Andrews Plain, opposite the old Blackfriars monastery. (If you feel like walking a bit further, turn left down London Street and at the bottom you will see the ancient market place, recently renovated, and immediately facing you the ancient Guildhall, completed in its original form in the mid-15th century; the Pastons would have been familiar with it as both lawyers and plaintiffs.)

¶ At St Andrew's Plain cross the road and turn right up the narrow Princes Street to St Peter Hungate, no longer used as a church but once the church that John Paston's body rested in on the long journey to Bromholm priory. *The nave and transepts were totally rebuilt, as 'a neat building of black flints' by John and Margaret Paston in 1458, after they had acquired the advowson (the right to appoint an incumbent) from St Mary's College. A stone in a buttress near the north door records this – it shows a tree trunk without branches (= decay of the old church) with a new shoot (= the new building), together with the date of completion – 1460.*

¶ At St Peter Hungate turn left down Elm Hill to the Monastery car park.

ST PETER HUNGATE CHURCH, WHERE
RESTED JOHN PASTON'S BODY ON ITS WAY
TO BROMHOLM. INSET: THE PASTON 'TREE'.

The Guildhall

The Pastons would have known the Guildhall at Norwich rather well, both as lawyers and as plaintiffs. According to 18th-century historian Francis Blomefield, 'in 1407, John Daniel, Robert Brasier and 22 more were elected to consult how to raise money to build the Guildhall'.

Master mason John Marowe was first to be hired, then Walter Daniel and Robert Dunston were elected to supervise. A total of 24 people were authorised to raise taxes and press citizens to work 'every day from 5 o'clock in the morning to 8 at night'. This was not as draconian as it sounds – in medieval times there was a tradition of willing communal co-operation on major works. Progress was swift, with work soon starting on the second storey. Work began in 1407 to house courts and prisoners, plus space for accounts, tax collectors and record storage. Within two years the roof was on; three years later the prisoners went in. Work went on until 1453.

It was made from flint rubble faced with knapped flints laid in mortar and packed with flint chippings. The Guildhall was so good it lasted for centuries, though the exterior

THE GUILDHALL REQUIRES A DETOUR INTO THE MARKET PLACE.

was reconstructed in 1861. Magistrates sat there until 1977, and prisoners were housed as late as 1980. It had three chambers big enough for court rooms. Its design was influenced by the Low Countries, with whose great merchant cities Norwich was linked economically and culturally. For a century all was well, but in 1511 the roof of the Mayor's Court collapsed. Its design may have been

to blame. Maybe the undercroft of the old toll house was inadequate to bear the weight above it.

On the first floor were two main halls used for council meetings and court rooms. The larger assembly chamber had a long room with a dais at the end opposite the door and a private room behind.

Brampton to Oxnead and Burgh next Aylsham

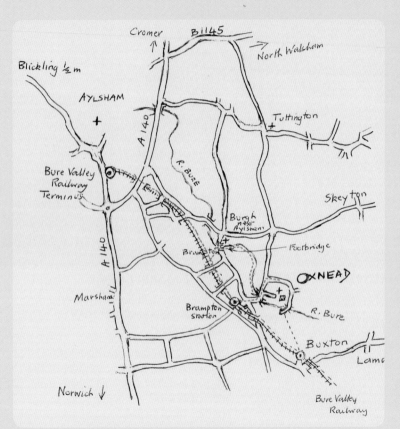

One of the joys of this particular walk is the discovery of beautiful, quiet corners only reachable if you will leave the car behind and look for small treasures rather than big tourist attractions. There can be few more beautiful places in North Norfolk than the little church at Oxnead or the unusual and unexpected interior of Burgh next Aylsham church. Combine these with the joys of watching the trout swim in the gentle river Bure or walking through water meadows thick with wild flowers and insects – and even the humbler pleasures of feeding the ducks – and you have the recipe for a perfect day's outing (dependent on weather and season of course!).

Another joy is leaving your car behind and taking the train! There is little room to park at either Oxnead or Burgh next Aylsham, so the best way to do the walk, if time permits, is to catch the Bure Valley railway trains at either Aylsham or Wroxham (the Wroxham trains connect with Norwich) and alight at Brampton station.

¶ From the station walk down to the crossroads in a north-easterly direction and continue over and down to the bridge over the river Bure. *The mill can be seen on your right as you cross the bridge. Oxnead church entrance is a little way over the bridge and to your right up a track. It is alongside Oxnead Hall – you'll see it over the wall. Only the kitchen wing of the Pastons' old hall remains.*

Oxnead was a Paston property from about 1421, when it was purchased by Sir William Paston, but it was not a major Paston house until Clement Paston (younger brother of Erasmus Paston of Paston Hall, who died in 1538) became an admiral.

Inside Oxnead church, a simple nave and chancel next to the Hall, are several Paston monuments, notably a Tudor monument to Clement Paston, who died in 1597, and his widow, who is buried in front of the altar beneath a fine stone slab with brass armorials; her son lies beside her. There are several smaller Paston monuments.

TOMB OF CLEMENT PASTON, IN OXNEAD CHURCH.

The following walk is short and beautiful but a bit muddy near the river, especially in winter!

¶ Go back to the bridge and join the river footpath on the south side. The footpath meanders along the river and down to Burgh next Aylsham about two miles away. From there it winds around to rejoin the railway line where you can turn either towards Aylsham or back towards Brampton, rejoining the train there as the walk follows the railway line in both directions.

¶ When you see the church of Burgh next Aylsham in the distance, take the time to cross the bridge and look inside. *It has one of the most beautiful and unusual restored Early English interiors (built 1375) in any of North Norfolk's medieval churches. The tiled floor and plain windows hold the light, giving a sense of sanctuary and peace. There is a fine example of a seven sacraments font.*

BURGH CHURCH

Oxnead and the later Pastons

Sir Clement Paston transformed Oxnead from a minor Paston estate to the finest of all their properties, but he died without heir in 1597; the estate passed to Sir William Paston, builder of the great barn at Paston and of the school at North Walsham. When he in turn died in 1610, the estates went to his grandson, Sir Edmund Paston, and then to his son William, who married Lady Katherine Bertie. They set up home at Oxnead and over the next few years became chief patrons of the arts in Norfolk. Chimney pieces, balconies, statues, ornaments and pictures embellished the beautiful Tudor house. Nicholas Stone made statues of Venus and Cupid, Jupiter, Flora and Cerberus for the garden and an iron pergola embellished with eight gilded balls. But in 1637, Lady Katherine died in childbirth, bearing their sixth child, and the dream was shattered. Nicholas Stone recorded he was commissioned to make 'a tomb for my Lady Katren, his dear wyef'. The bust of Lady Katherine still gazes over the church, clearly a portrait; she seems forever young and rather ordinary – raised to extraordinary honour by the love of her husband. William Paston travelled abroad after serving as Lord Lieutenant of the county. He returned from Italy and Eygpt in 1639 and resumed life at Oxnead.

The shadow of Civil War was looming over the country and Paston was nearly alone amongst the gentry of Norfolk in supporting the royalist cause. He was made Earl of Yarmouth in 1641 and came to London in 1642 to 'avoid employment' by parliament as a leader of militia. In 1643, like many royalist supporters in East Anglia, he slipped across to Holland. He had no military experience and no militia as Parliament had taken his men from him. He must have felt that a gentleman of means but no experience in war could better support the king overseas. The estates of the Pastons were then sequestered and £1,100 of plate from Oxnead was sent to help the Roundheads. In 1644 William Paston came home and, in return for lavish fines, was allowed to stay at Oxnead. The Paston properties and wealth never recovered. He died in 1663 at Oxnead but there is no memorial to him in the church.

His son, Robert, held office as Lord Lieutenant of Norfolk and served as an MP. He continued the tradition of enriching and embellishing Oxnead and entertained Charles II there. He was made Earl of Yarmouth in 1679 and died in 1683.

In the 1670s Robert commissioned the poignant painting known as *The Yarmouth Collection* (or as *The Paston Treasure*). This is in the Castle Museum at Norwich. In it the artist shows a fraction of the collections amassed at Oxnead all jumbled together like a magnificent car boot sale. Gold and silver are mixed with shells and curiosities from around the world – Robert was a founder member of the Royal Society and very interested in scientific discovery. A globe is turned to the East Indies, where the Pastons may well have invested. A young slave is in the background and a parrot and a monkey show the wealth of interests the Pastons claimed. But in the middle is a portrait of his daughter, probably Mary Paston, who died in 1676. She holds roses, a symbol of the transience of life, and her songbook. The only legible words in this are on the subject of death. Sir Robert wrote: 'All is so uncertain in this world that no man knows which way to turn'. He must have known his financial situation was precarious when he commissioned the painting; it is an eloquent elegy for the family that amassed wealth and riches and influence from nothing – and in three hundred years returned to nothing. Perhaps the meaning is simply that in the face of loss, possessions no longer matter. (An excellent detailed evaluation of the symbolism of this picture can be found on the Castle Museum's website.)

His son, also William Paston, had a much lower profile in Norfolk life, inheriting debts and out of favour when William and Mary acceded to the throne, he had to sell his estates. It was said that he had 'scarce a servant to attend him or a horse to ride upon'. He died in 1732 with no male heir.

The estate was sold to Lord Anson together with Paston Hall when the second Earl of Yarmouth went bankrupt. It was from here that the Paston letters were sold to Peter le Neve, an antiquary, to help meet his debts.

John Adey Repton, a long-term tenant at the hall, sent a drawing of the hall to an antiquarian, writing:

Oxnead Hall, with the two terraces, must have had a very magnificent appearance: the principal front, shewn in the sketch, faces the south, whilst the buildings on the west side contain offices. The centre is appropriated to the hall and chapel and in the eastern side is a ballroom, gallery and apartments for the family. At the end was a lofty building with sash windows called the banqueting room, which was built by the first Earl of Yarmouth to receive Charles II . . . The fountain and statues which stood on the platform, are still to be seen in Blickling Park near Aylsham. Some of the old inhabitants say, that under the banqueting room was a vaulted apartment which they called the frisketting room, probably from the Italian 'frescati', a cool grotto.

The Paston connection

The Pastons eventually owned or had influence on the following sites in Norfolk:

1. Paston Hall, lands and almshouse
2. Gimingham Lancaster
3. Trunch
4. Knapton
5. North Walsham
6. Bacton
7. Cromer (through Agnes Paston)
8. Gresham Castle
9. Caister Castle (through Sir John Fastolf)
10. Fritton
11. Drayton
12. Hellesdon
13. Cotton
14. Guton
15. Mautby (by marriage to Margaret Paston)
16. Sparham
17. Marlingford
18. Great Cressingham
19. Briston
20. East Beckham
21. Somerton
22. Swainsthorpe
23. Winterton Ness
24. Framlingham Castle, Suffolk – seat of the Dukes of Norfolk. Here young John Paston III was sent as a page to establish good relations with the ducal family after the re-taking of Caister in 1461
25. Wingfield Manor, Suffolk – main East Anglian seat of the dukes of Suffolk
26. Elm Hill, Norwich – probably the house built by Augustus Steward (marked by a blue plaque)
27. Norwich, King Street – Paston House, now known as the Music House, bought by John Paston III in 1487
28. Norwich. St Peter Hungate Church was repaired and rebuilt by John and Margaret Paston in 1460.
29. Norwich, St. Andrew's Hall. The arms of John Paston and Margaret Mautby are carved on the great south door as benefactors to the Dominican friars
30. Paston Sixth Form College, North Walsham, founded by William Paston
31. Thorpe Hall, owned by the Appleton Pastons, was sold in 1670
32. Oxnead Hall
33. Appleton Hall (now Flitcham cum Appleton). Burnt to the ground with the family in bed inside. Never rebuilt.
34. Barningham Hall. Still standing!
35. Baconsthorpe Castle (by marriage to Bridget Heydon)
36. Felbrigg: Erasmus married Mary Wyndham of Felbrigg Hall
37. Oxburgh. Margaret Paston of Appleton married Sir Henry Bedingfeld, 1st baronet of Oxburgh, in 1661; Margaret Paston II married Sir Henry Bedingfeld, 6th baronet, in 1826. He then changed the family name to Paston-Bedingfeld.

They also owned houses in London where they stayed when visiting Court.

Oxburgh Hall

Although the elder branch of the Paston family died out with the death of William Paston, 2nd Earl of Yarmouth, the Paston family continued in the direct line, that of Edward Paston of Appleton. Edward Paston was the son of Thomas Paston, a younger son of William Paston and Bridget Heydon. In 1539 he bought Binham Priory from Henry VIII both for the land and for the building materials. He failed to build a house at Binham but used the materials to build at Appleton. His son Edward was a godson of Edward VI, whose short reign brought Protestantism to England in a much more revolutionary form than Henry VIII had conceived. Edward, ironically, became a Catholic and was consequently not popular in court circles.

Edward Paston, born 1550, as a godson of Edward VI could have had a glittering (if dangerous) career at court. Instead, he became a collector of music and a patron of the arts. His tomb at Blofield celebrates his love of 'liberall sciences, especially musicke and poetry as also strange languages'. He was a patron of Byrd and a friend of Philip Sidney. He rebuilt Appleton in 1612 but neither the hall nor the church survives – the Pastons had very little luck with their buildings. One wonders if he enjoyed the hospitality of the rival hall of the sciences and arts at Oxnead.

The Wars of the Roses

The Paston letters cover the reigns of six English kings. At this period, the Plantagenet family (also known as the House of York, being descendants of Edmund, Duke of York, and symbolised by a white rose) supplied three English kings and also claimed the throne of France. The English maintained a garrison at Calais and John Paston was stationed there. The House of Lancaster was descended from John of Gaunt, Duke of Lancaster (brother of Edmund, Duke of York), and represented by a red rose. The Wars of the Roses (1455–87) were the struggle between these two families for the throne of England; they ended after Henry VII (of Lancaster, but married to Elizabeth of York) won the Battle of Bosworth in 1485 and united the two warring families.

John Paston II was in the king's household while his brother John III served in the household of the Duke of Norfolk. Both travelled extensively and found it expensive. Here John II pleads with his father for understanding:

May it please you to understand the great expense I have travelling with the King . . .

and how I am ordered to have my horse and harness ready at haste . . . In especial I beseech you that I may have some money before Easter.

The only battle of the Wars of the Roses on Norfolk soil was the siege of Caister castle and that was (arguably) more about property in Norfolk and envy of an upstart lawyer, John Paston, than about the English throne.

Until the Battle of Bosworth in 1485, it was common for the King to issue a pardon (for a small fee) to the lesser nobility that fought against them. One of the confusions for modern readers is that the Pastons then simply refer to the King, i.e. the one at present in office. They seem to have been fairly happy with any king. More important was the patronage of the Earl of Oxford. The Duke of Norfolk was far more important than either. Here William writes to his brother John III about the King's forthcoming visit to Norwich in 1487:

As for the King's coming into the country, on Monday fortnight he will lie at the Abbey of Stratford and so to Chelmsford . . . then to Hedingham [seat of the Earls of Oxford], then to Colchester, then to Ipswich, then to Bury, then to Dame Anne Wingfield's [at East Harling] and so to Norwich. He will be there on the eve of Palm Sunday and so tarry there all Easter and then go to Walsingham. Wherefore you need to warn William Gogyne and his fellows to provide themselves with enough wine, as everyone assures me the town will be drunk dry, as York was when the King was there.

Master Sampson sends word that . . . my sister [Margery, John's wife] with all goodly folk from around there should come with Dame Calthorpe at the King's coming, because there is no great lady around there and my Lord has made great boast about the fair and good gentlewomen of the country, and the King has said he would like to see them . . . Your country is greatly boasted of, and also its inhabitants.

Pilgrimage

The idea of a 'journey with a meaning' lies deep within our identity and also is well evidenced in our literature. From the Canterbury Tales, through *The Pilgrim's Progress* and on to *The Lord of the Rings* the quest has been a way of understanding our search for meaning in life. Pilgrimage was this special journey in the 15th century and there are plenty of references to these journeys in the Paston letters. We know that it was open to all classes (although poorer people might go on a journey to a shrine in England rather than abroad) – Margery Kempe of King's Lynn went on pilgrimages to Rome and Santiago and she was a butcher's wife. All England's kings in the 15th century came to Walsingham and the Duke of Norfolk journeyed there barefoot in 1457.

Stow chapel, on the hill where the windmill now stands in Paston, is at a junction of the road to Bromholm and the old road to Great Yarmouth. Mr Bardswell, a descendant of the Mack family of Paston, showed me some research he did on the cross at Stow chapel (found in pieces in a rockery at the mill in 1920) and the crosses at Southrepps and at Gresham. He thought they marked an old pilgrim route from Bromholm to Walsingham. Stow chapel was almost certainly a rest chapel for pilgrims – it is at the top of a hill, steep for Norfolk! – but after the Reformation its stones were reused in local buildings. Similarly, the stone to build the great barns of Paston and Waxham came from St Benet's at Holme and Bromholm priory and Thomas Paston purchased Binham Priory in 1539 in order to build his fine new home.

Chaucer's famous pilgrims left for Canterbury nearly a century before the Pastons wrote of their own journeys but it is clear that then, as now, this special journey created a bond between people with a common purpose.

Margaret writes that she will go to St Leonard's and Walsingham to pray for John's recovery – by this time Bromholm had lost popularity as a place of pilgrimage but St Leonard's, on the edge of Mousehold heath (about where the gas tower now stands) was very popular.

What was required of the pilgrim? The sacrifice of time and often money: Margaret says that *my mother promised another image of wax the weight of you to our Lady of Walsingham, and she sent four nobles to the four orders of Friars at Norwich to pray for you.*

John III went all the way to Santiago in 1473 on pilgrimage and this was accepted as a reasonable and wise journey by his family.

What did the pilgrim receive? In a world where treacle was a great medicine and violent crime was ever close to home, where much was uncertain, faith and the certainty of forgiveness, the hope of eternity and the shared beliefs of society must have been a valuable and treasured resource. Those

THIS INSCRIPTION OVER THE DOOR OF PASTON GREAT BARN APPEARS TO INDICATE THAT THE STONE CAME FROM BROMHOLM PRIORY.

who have no need will not take a pilgrimage because the point is that it should cost the pilgrim – the more the better – not necessarily money, but certainly the time to think and pray. A pilgrimage was often taken for a specific request, as Margaret's was, sometimes to search for forgiveness or reconciliation. It was a known and valued remedy for the physical and spiritual ills of life and also 'time out'. At this time, for many, the only holidays were Holy Days – of which there were many as the headings of the letters show. A pilgrimage was a reason to go on a journey, to explore new ways. Hospitality would be found on all the old pilgrimage routes, and, if you wanted companionship or protection, there would be fellow pilgrims. A pilgrim badge could protect you on the journey as the extract from the letter on sea travel shows.

'Pilgrimage takes hold of you in ways you never expected. It becomes part of you, or you become part of it.' So says one of the pilgrims in David Dickinson's novel *Death of a Pilgrim*. We don't share the cultural understanding of a pilgrimage as Margaret Paston would have seen it but we still make our journeys, through time, to special places often in England now forgotten or neglected, and they are still important to us – even if we don't, altogether, know why.

St Leonard's Priory, Norwich

The priory of St Leonard was built by Bishop Herbert on a hill near the city of Norwich, in Thorpwood, for the accommodation of several Benedictine monks, while the Cathedral Church and Priory were in course of erection. It was afterwards continued as a cell of the great monastery under the rule of a prior appointed by the prior of Norwich and confirmed by the bishop. The prior of St Leonard's had to account annually to his superior for all the offerings in the priory church of St Leonard, as well as for those of the adjacent chapel of St Michael on the Mount, which was served by the monks.

Blomefield states that the church of this priory was noted for a famous image of King Henry VI, which attracted many pilgrims, 'so that the offerings to this good king and the images of the Holy Virgin, the Holy Cross, and St Anthony brought in a good round annual sum'. It is rather curious to note that, under the elaborate accounts of the Cathedral Priory in the Valor Ecclesiasticus (1535), the only offerings named in connection with the church of this cell are those that were made at the image of St Leonard; and they merely amounted to 6½d in 1534.

HENRY VI.

At the dissolution of the monasteries, the site and demesnes of this priory were granted to Thomas, Duke of Norfolk.

North Walsham and beyond

One of the earliest references to relations between the Paston family and the small market town of North Walsham is this one, found in Blomefield's history of Norfolk:

About the year 1413 Clement Paston, esq, John Horningtoft of Paston, merchant, Laurence de Thorp and John Parson of Edingthorpe, came to this town (North Walsham), entered into the pasture etc of the abbott belonging to his manor, with their cattle, fed and trod it down to the damage of 40s, fished his ponds, etc and took 200 roaches, 200 perch, and 300 eels, to the value of 100s and carried them away, but by what authority we do not know.

It is a curious incident, particularly as Clement Paston died in 1417 – he wasn't a young lad stealing fish but a respected country gentleman. And what did they use to catch so many fish and take them away? Why did they want them?

The Abbot referred to is the Abbot of St Benet's at Holme. This was a Benedictine foundation, founded as early as AD 800, reputedly by a Saxon named Suneman. The Danes destroyed the abbey in AD 870 but it was rebuilt by King Cnut (Canute). By the 15th century, this abbey had 34 churches, 51 lordships and manors, lands, tithes and services in 111 parishes in Norfolk. Clement apparently had '5 or 6 score acre of land at most'.

It was certainly hard for the Pastons to prove title and to keep their lands with such powerful neighbours.

Paston (William) recommends himself to your good lordship, willing with all his heart to do you service. And as touching the manor of Walsham, he says that he will show you and prove that this manor and all the lands and crops this year are his own truly by title in law and conscience.

The Paston letters mention many of the villages around North Walsham which, like Walsham itself, were the property of the Abbots of St Benets. Did Clement Paston feel squeezed between the Prior of Bromholm to the south of the parish and the Abbot to the west? There were also the family properties of John of Gaunt, whose descendants owned the estates to the north – they were the mighty Dukes of Lancaster. It must have seemed so unlikely at the time that one of Clement's descendants should marry into the Beaufort family and become a relation of the Lancasters. The Pastons at that time were more on a level with the smaller landowners in the villages and they owed their living to growing barley, rearing flocks of sheep and keeping the law on their side. Local pride in the goods of their own country shine through in this excerpt from William Paston (1378–1444) writing to his cousin Robert:

I pray that you will send me hither two ells [an ell was 45 inches (1.14m)] of Worsted for doublets, to happen [wrap me up warm] this cold winter, and that ye enquire where William Paston bought his tippet of fine worsted cloth, which is almost like silk, and if that be much finer than that ye should buy me, after seven or eight shillings, then buy me a quarter and a nail [13¼ inches (34cm)] thereof for collars, though it be dearer than the others, for I shall make my doublet all Worsted, for the glory of Norfolk.

Worstead, home of worsted cloth, was also part of the lands of St Benet's.

Sir William Paston's School

The prestige of the Paston family had grown throughout the 16th century. Erasmus Paston married Margaret, daughter of Sir Thomas Windham of Felbrigg, and their son William was born in 1528. He would enjoy a long life of 82 years.

In 1546 William went to study at Gonville Hall in Cambridge. Marrying Frances, daughter of Sir Thomas Clere of Stokesby, he then inherited most of the estates from his grandfather and then in the last years of the century he inherited the Oxnead estates from his uncle, Clement Paston.

He became Sir William in 1578 but contented himself with management of his estates in the county and with his work as a magistrate; he was known for his liberality. This would find its greatest expression in his endowment of a school at North Walsham.

Charles Forder, historian of the school, comments that Sir William very much intended to control his own school during his lifetime. Sir William's own links with Gonville and Caius colleges at university would be seen in the number of students that would

go from the school to those colleges. Forder also outlines how the building of the first school building came about after the devastating fire which burned down much

of the centre and south of North Walsham in 1600. Sir William purchased a plot of the devastated land and two years later plans were well advanced. Sir William was intimately involved in the drawing up of the Deed of Foundation in 1604, a deed which hangs on the wall of the Paston Sixth Form College today. The school actually opened in that year but legal processes to ensure the continuing financial stability of the school continued and Sir William's final 'Deed of Gift' was signed on 1st October 1606, the day which the school would celebrate annually.

Over the years many of the youth of the gentry of north-east Norfolk would attend the school and then a much wider group of young men would have the opportunity to become students there. The alumni would soon include clerics from parish priests to an archbishop, academics, antiquarians and men of the army and navy. Of these, Admiral

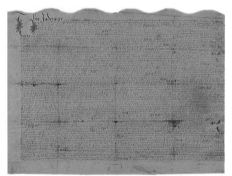

SIR WILLIAM PASTON'S DEED OF GIFT, DATED 1606, BY WHICH HE FOUNDED THE COLLEGE WHICH STILL BEARS HIS NAME

Horatio Lord Nelson is the most famous. He and his brother William were transferred from school in Norwich to the North Walsham school when it seemed to be enjoying a period of considerable reputation and it was direct from the school that Nelson entered the navy.

The story of Sir William's school is available in full in Charles Forder's history; in the 20th century it would operate as part of the county school system and under the formal 'grammar school' structure, with selection by the 11 plus examination. In 1983 the then governors had to make the difficult decision to become a sixth form only establishment and the girls of the North Walsham High School also became 'Pastonians'. With Sir William's original 40

students now a very successful college of more than 600 students, his original intent of a high quality, broad and liberal education for the young people of north and east Norfolk is certainly fulfilled.

Paston Sixth Form College is today a very busy working college. Nelson's schoolroom can still be visited by arrangement; a contemporary painting of the founder by an unknown artist continues to look down in the Principal's study. Varnish hides much of the detail in the picture but Sir William continues to observe the education process which he began. The College celebrated the first 400 years of the Foundation with a ball on the school lawn in 2006.

Sir William Paston's tomb

As the century turned in 1600, Sir William Paston was 72 years old and thinking of his legacy. The school that would bear his name over the centuries would be the encompassing legacy, for the benefit of the families of his home county. His personal legacy, the symbol by which he wished men and women to remember him in the future, would be a fine tomb in the great church of St Nicholas in North Walsham. There would even be instructions to the students at his school to attend at the church and remember him through this very prominent memorial. In the 20th century, boys of the Paston School would annually walk past his tomb at the Founders' Day service.

Sir William would take matters still further. He would not rest content with instructing that a prominent tomb must be erected; he wanted to see that the job was done properly and see the tomb himself. Thus it was that he drew up a contract with two tradesmen in London for the work. The contract was quite specific on every part of the tomb, the types of stone, the epitaphs, the pillars and the coats of arms.

North Walsham church has much to interest the visitor – the great east window, a memorial to the fallen in the First World War, the town chest, various coats of arms – and an audio tour is available to the visitor.

Cromer and other Paston estates

Cromer would be a great place to rest and recover while undertaking the long distance Paston walk as it is where the Paston Way meets the North Norfolk Coastal path. From our point of view, more importantly, one of the Cromer manors was among Agnes Paston's manors that she brought to her marriage with William Paston. Here her grandson makes sure it is looked after while he is away:

Also, mother I pray my brother Edmond may ride to Marlingford, Oxnead, Paston and Cromer and in all these manors go in my name, also let the tenants at Oxnead and Marlingford know that I sent no word to him to take money from them.

Marlingford was in dispute as William, John's uncle, thought he had a better right to it. It looks as if Cromer and Paston had no luck on that occasion and had to pay. The manor of Ropers in Cromer was left to Agnes for life by William and presumably then reverted to her grandsons as her son predeceased her. Walter Rye (*Cromer Past and Present*) briefly mentions the manor of Ropers at Cromer but not where it lies. However in Agnes Paston's will of 1466, she states her life interest as

being in the manors of 'Paston, Latymer, and Shipden, and Ropers in Cromer', so the family clearly had extensive interests there. The plot thickens as in 1544, Sir William Paston settled Cromer Weylands to the use of his wife Bridget and himself for life and afterwards to the use of his will. Like Paston itself, this manor was then bought by George Anson with the sale of all the Paston lands that were left to the last Earl of Yarmouth.

On 2nd July 1426 Sir William Paston as Lord of the manor of 'Shippedene' (Cromer) obtained a confirmation by Letters Patent of the market and fair granted to Nicholas de Weylond in 1285, so one small remnant of the influence of the Pastons remains.

Cromer would have been a strategic holding for the Pastons. It was the biggest port between Blakeney and Wells to the west and Yarmouth to the south and the sea was vital for traders. It was far easier to travel with large quantities of goods by sea than by land – but not always safer: Margaret writes to John in 1450:

There have been many enemies against Yarmouth and Cromer, and they have done much harm and taken many Englishmen and put them in great distress and held them to ransom. These enemies are so bold they come up to the land and play on Caister sands and in other places as much at home as if they were Englishmen. Folks have been right sore afeared that they will do much harm this summer.

Fears of danger from the sea are also apparent in this letter from Agnes to John in 1449 about the pirates near Mundesley:

And as you send me no tidings I send you such as be in this country: Richard Lynstead came this day from Paston and let me know that, on Saturday last past, Dravell was taken by enemies, walking by the seaside, and they took two pilgrims, a man and a woman, and they robbed the woman and let her go, and led the man to the sea; and when they knew he was a pilgrim, they gave him money and put him again on land; and they have taken four ships this week off Winterton, and Happisburgh and Eccles.

But the sea gave to the Pastons as well: they had 'right of wreck', a valuable privilege in

SOMEWHERE UNDER MODERN CROMER, OR MAYBE UNDER THE SEA, LIE FIELDS ONCE OWNED BY THE PASTON FAMILY. IN THEIR DAY CROMER MERCHANTS WERE EXPORTING GRAIN AND IMPORTING FISH AND BALTIC TIMBER – MAKING ENOUGH MONEY DOING SO TO BUILD A CHURCH WITH THE TALLEST TOWER IN NORFOLK.

manors by the sea. This is what was carried away from one ship at Winterton that was wrecked on Paston land.

Twenty two cartsfull of stuff, eight score bow staves, three score and seven score planks, fourteen hundred clapboards (for making casks), five barrels of tar, four pairs of oars, and great plenty of wreck.

Such free materials were a valuable perk for seaside villages. At Paston, even up to the 1950s, families would go with an old pram or cart to the beach each Sunday to see what they could pick up.

But then life was dangerous on land as well. This is part of an anonymous statement giving information of local outrages:

Robert Ledham and his men . . . in the church of Birlingham set on two of the servants of the Bishop of Norwich when they were kneeling at Mass. And then and there they would have killed them . . . six of them assaulted John Paston at the doors of the Cathedral with swords and daggers, one of them holding the said Paston by both arms at his back . . . and smote one of the servants on the naked head by the sword, polluting the sanctuary.

The Pastons also owned land at Trunch and, as usual, had trouble collecting the rent.

Again, Agnes uses Edmund for this; did she prefer him to his older brothers and so leave him her manor at Cromer, or was this his role in the family business?

I advise you to think every day of your fathers counsel to learn the law, for he said many times that those who dwell at Paston will have need to defend themselves . . . There is a man at Trunch called Palmer that had land at Trunch for seven years from your father and had paid all those years and now he has paid 8s to Gimingham which your father never paid. Geoffrey asked Palmer why the rent was not paid in mine husbands time; and Palmer said, for he was a great man, and a wise man of law, and that was the cause men would not ask him the rent.

Collecting tenants' money was undoubtedly hard work in those times and there was a high risk of refusal – if tenants thought a mightier lord might protect them or also demand money claiming that the land was theirs. Dogged persistence was required and careful attention to all the many scattered manors that the Pastons owned.

In the face of these difficulties it is amazing that so many letters got through without trouble. It was important to write when a messenger was available as sometimes it might be several weeks before another

chance came; Sir John Paston here complains that he has had no news:

I marvel that you send me no writing since you departed, I heard no news out of Norfolk since that time. You might at St Bartholomews fair have had messengers enough for London.

Fairs and markets offered the chance of sending a letter by a messenger but it was important to choose carefully. As Margaret complains:

I could not get a messenger . . . unless I sent by the Sheriffs men; but I knew not their master nor them or if they were enemies to you or not.

A special message would be carried by one of the Paston servants – but there was no guarantee how long it would take to reach its destination. A journey by fast messenger on horseback might take only a day to reach Norwich from Paston but such a messenger might meet with bad weather, robbers or bad roads. Sometimes the messenger would wait to return with the answer. But even the best were fallible. John Paston writes:

God help me, I sent you a letter to London after Candlemas, by a man of my Lord's; and he forgot to deliver it to you, and so he brought to me the letter again.

A really long walk

When the Paston family were sending their letters up and down the country they sometimes had to wait a long time for an answer, depending on the messenger they could find to carry the letter. While sometimes the messenger was on horseback, sometimes the deliverer of the letter walked. This is a suggestion for a long walk around Norfolk using the network of long distance paths we are so lucky to have. Full directions for the long distance paths mentioned can be found on the websites detailed at the back of the book.

¶ Start at Great Yarmouth (taking time to explore this historic town) and take Weavers Way through the Halvergate marshes and over the railway line at Berney; the path then takes you up through Thurne and Acle and on to North Walsham. *You will pass north of Worstead and through Meeting Hill where John Paston's body is reputed to have been carried across the ford on his way to Bromholm for burial (see A Funeral Feast).*

¶ Leave Weavers Way at North Walsham and visit Sir William Paston's tomb in the church in the market place. From here, join the Griffon area walk to Pigney's Wood by crossing the Vicarage Road car park behind the church to find the entrance. At Pigney's Wood you will now be on the walk from North Walsham to Paston described in this guidebook (see page 28).

¶ From St Margaret's church in Paston, take the walk from Paston to Mundesley and join the Paston Way at the junction of Craft Lane. The Paston Way will lead you pleasantly to Cromer where you can join the Norfolk coast path. Follow this as far as Holme-next-the-sea and take Peddars Way which leads directly to Castle Acre priory. Peddars Way now continues towards Thetford but you may wish to take a detour to Oxburgh Hall. *This route takes you through Broadland and up to the beautiful area of outstanding natural beauty on the coast that extends right along the Norfolk coast path, then down through the quiet villages of the west of the county, through Breckland and to Thetford forest. It is a beautiful way to discover Paston Country if you are blessed with plenty of time and energy.*

OXBURGH HALL

THE TOMB OF SIR EDMUND PASTON (DIED 1632) IN PASTON CHURCH. HIS MEMORY WAS REVERED IN THIS IMPOSING MARBLE TOMB BY NICHOLAS STONE, THE LEADING MONUMENTAL SCULPTOR OF THE DAY.

Further Reading

Editions of the Paston Letters

Original Letters, written during the reigns of Henry VI., Edward IV., and Richard III., by various persons of rank or consequence ed. John Fenn (5 vols. London, 1787–1823) – the original antiquarian edition

Illustrated Letters of the Paston Family: Private Life in the Fifteenth Century ed. Roger Virgoe (London: Macmillan, 1989) – out of print but good copies can be found on the Internet

Paston Letters and Papers of the Fifteenth Century ed. Norman Davis (2 vols. Oxford: Clarendon Press, 1971–76) – this scholarly edition, in the original spelling, is being made available online by the Universty of Virginia Library <http://etext.lib.virginia.edu/toc/modeng/public/PasLett.htlm>

The Paston Letters: a Selection in Modern Spelling ed. Norman Davis (Oxford: Oxford University Press, 1983, World's Classics series)

General Background

Richard Barber, *The Pastons: A Family in the Wars of the Roses* (London: Folio Society, 1981; reissued by Penguin in 1984 and by the Boydell Press in 1993)

H. S. Bennett, *The Pastons and their England: Studies in an Age of Transition* (2nd ed. Cambridge: Cambridge University Press, 1932)

Francis Blomefield, *An Essay towards a Topographical History of the County of Norfolk* ed. Charles Parkin (11 vols. London, 1805–10)

Helen Castor, *Blood and Roses: the Paston Family in the Fifteenth Century* (London: Faber, 2004)

J. G. Coad and Glyn Coppack, *Castle Acre Castle and Priory, Norfolk* (London: English Heritage, 1998)

Charles Forder, *A History of the Paston School* (2nd ed. North Walsham: Paston School, 1980)

Henry Harrod, *Gleanings among the Castles and Convents of Norfolk* (Norwich, 1857)

R. W. Ketton-Cremer, *Norfolk Assembly* (London: Faber, 1957) – includes material on Sir William Paston

Herbert Loraine, *Paston: Some Notes on the Church of St. Margaret and the Paston Family* (North Walsham: Rounce & Wortley, 1949)

Marjorie Mack, *The Educated Pin* (London: Faber & Faber, 1944) – autobiographical account of life in Paston village by a descendant of the Paston family

Oxburgh Hall, Norfolk (London: National Trust, 1990)

David C. Price, *Patrons and Musicians of the English Renaissance* (Cambridge: Cambridge University Press, 1981)

Colin Richmond, *The Paston Family in the Fifteenth Century* (3 vols. Cambridge: Cambridge University Press, 1990–2001)

Bruce Robinson, *Walking the Norfolk Long Distance Trail: The Coast Path* (Cromer: Poppyland, 2006)

Dawson Turner, *Sketch of the History of Caister Castle, near Yarmouth, including Biographical Notices of Sir J. Fastolfe, and of Different Individuals of the Paston Family* (London & Great Yarmouth, 1842)

Websites

A website specifically linked to this book can be found at <www.poppyland.co.uk> – follow the 'Support and Resources' link.

All websites are correct at time of going to press. The sites are offered for your information and neither Poppyland Publishing nor the authors of this book take any responsibility for content.

Baconsthorpe Castle
  <www.english-heritage.org.uk>
Bacton woods
  <www.forestry.gov.uk>
Bure Valley Railway
  <www.bvrw.co.uk>
Dragon Hall
  <www.dragonhall.org>
Caister Castle
  <www.caistercastle.co.uk>
Castle Acre Priory
  <www.english-heritage.org.uk>
Elm Hill
  <www.elmhill.co.uk>
Griffon Area Partnership *(walks maps)*
  <www.griffon.org.uk>
Norfolk churches
  <www.norfolkchurches.co.uk>
Norfolk Coast
  <www.norfolkcoastaonb.org.uk>
Norfolk Coast path
  <www.nationaltrail.co.uk>
Norwich
  <www.heritagecity.org>
  <www.visitnorwich.co.uk>
Norwich Castle Museum
  <www.museums.norfolk.gov.uk>
Norwich Cathedral
  <www.cathedral.org.uk>

Oxburgh Hall
  <www.nationaltrust.org.uk>
Paston
  <www.pastonheritage.co.uk>
Paston Great Barn – for details of guided tours email <ashley.murray@naturalengland.org.uk>
Paston Way
  <www.ldwa.org.uk>
St Peter Hungate
  <www.hungate.org.uk>
Stow Mill
  <www.stowmill.co.uk>
Weavers Way
  <www.countrysideaccess.norfolk.gov.uk/long-distance>

Index

THE ARMS OF THE EARLS OF YARMOUTH